EVERYTHING

*From losing his Love to
finding God's Love*

JANINE CUMMINGS

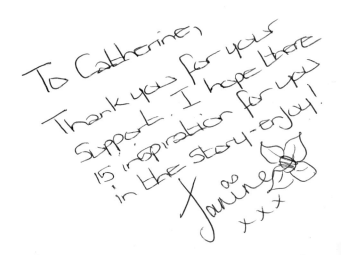

To Catherine,
Thank you for your
support. I hope there
is inspiration for you
in the story - enjoy!
Janine
xxx

Everything: From losing his Love to finding God's Love, Janine
Cummings.

Non Fiction Personal Life Story
All names of the real life characters featured in the story have been
changed to protect their identity.

Printed in the United Kingdom
First Printing: 2015.
ISBN 978-0-9932996-0-5

ABOUT THE AUTHOR

Janine Cummings, born in 1978, is a British writer based in West London. She grew up with her mother and sister, and although she retained some contact with her father until her early teens, it was her West Indian mother, Eurmin Cummings, who was the driving single-parent force in her life.

In her early teens, she began writing short poems which she performed at open mic sessions, and later went on to pursue a career in events management. After being educated to GCSE standard, Janine decided against furthering her education and left her dreams of becoming a journalist.

Her career path took a dramatic change in 2012 when her passion for fitness led to becoming a Freelance Fitness Instructor, which has afforded her great success at a number of gyms across London.

As a keen fitness fanatic and a lover of people, she enjoys building new relationships and helping people overcome their personal struggles.

Janine is a Born Again Christian who gave her life to Christ in November 2013, and her faith has grown into a passion and desire to encourage and empower other women to grow in faith. She has a desire to see the hearts and attitudes of young women change, particularly in how they view and value themselves, which Janine firmly believes starts through a relationship with God.

She has now turned her life experiences into a point of reference that has reignited her passion for writing through her debut book, Everything.

Janinevcummings@gmail.com

This book is dedicated to the most important women in my life:

My mother Eurmin Cummings, my sister Paige Cummings, my best friend Karen Tingle-Joseph and my God-daughter Allysia Marie Tingle.

I will love you all the days of my life.

"If I had stopped back then, how would I be here today? If I stop now, where will I be tomorrow?"

-Mr K, *My Great Transition*

ACKNOWLEDGEMENTS

Firstly I would like to acknowledge and thank My Father, God the Almighty who is the author and finisher of my life. God has given me a new life in Christ and the strength to run my race to victory. Without Him I am nothing and through Him I am everything He has ordained me to be. I want to thank God for His constant and unrelenting love which has sustained me and given me a gift to be able to reach the hearts of His people. God's words speak healing and He has healed me through to completion – blessed be His holy name.

To my mother Eurmin, I want to thank you and say that I love you. You have been the one constant source of parental strength and support. You have always been a dominant force in my life one way or another, and I thank God for your life and for choosing you to give birth to me. Without you, I could not exist and through your own life experiences you have taught me what it means to survive through adversity and to grow in greater resilience and strength. Thank you for teaching me to be a strong woman, but also a woman who has a voice and one that should be heard. I will love you always.

To my grandmother Thelma, thank you for being the rock of our family. You lost your husband but you never lost your strength. When most women would have fallen apart with four children to look after, you continued to work hard and provide for your family. You are a true reflection of survival.

To my sister Paige, there are no words to describe how in love I am with you. Thank you for your constant support and love. You make me proud every day and I feel so blessed to have you in my life. Your generosity and kindness is limitless, and you encourage me to be a better woman. Thank you for standing by me through all things.

To Daniella Blechner, thank you from the very depth of my heart for your love, support and coaching through the publishing process. Not only have you been a great mentor but you have come to be one of my closest friends. A soul sister and a woman of excellence – I will forever celebrate who you are and support you on your own journey through this wonderful life that God has blessed you with. You have the ability to touch people and bring value to the lives of those you meet, and I say with great admiration that you are the epitome of a beautiful woman.

To Jack Hibbert, I thank you for your pastoral care, support and love. You have formed a solid part of my spiritual journey growing in Christ and I will forever be indebted to you for what you have done in my life. I will never forget any of our talks and meetings; your payers and the selfless giving of your time. You have been like an earthly father to me and I thank God for your life. I will never forget you.

Thank you to Cassius Frankson of Cassiusfphotography and Tayo Soyoye of ATS Graphics for the work that went into creating the cover design. You both understood my vision and helped bring it to life in a positive and encouraging way.

To my family and close friends – I thank you for sticking by me, especially those of you who were with me during the difficult times I have written about in this book. There were moments of great emotion, but your encouragement and steadfast love is what got me through.

To Danielle Brand, you were the pioneer. You paved the way to encourage many of us writers and authors to fulfil our dreams. You were the first person I shared my vision with and if it were not for our early conversations about writing, I may not have taken a step of faith to live my dream and write this book. I salute you.

Thank you.

TABLE OF CONTENTS

INTRODUCTION

What does 'everything' mean to you? When I began writing this
story I can honestly say now that the words began and ended in the
hands of another. I had placed my all in someone who could never
have met with my expectations, because as human beings we are
all fallible. We make promises with good intentions, but there are
times when each and every one of us will either fail or be failed by
another. The truth is we have all loved someone who did not love us
back in the same way and in turn, we have been loved by someone
who we did not love back equally; that is okay – feelings, wants and
intentions can change, but it is how we honour them that is vitally
important. With those changes then comes a choice for all involved,
but the biggest choice comes from those of us who are left behind
with a decision to give up or keep going when everything changes.

For me, initially the journey was one of rejection and
loss. I fell into a complete state of bereavement over the end of my
relationship. It felt as though not only had my relationship died but,
with the loss of my partner, part of me had died also. I struggled
to make sense of what felt like abandonment and couldn't focus on
anything else simply because my relationship had been the central
nervous system of my life.

When we fall into a belief system of incompletion once a
loved one departs from a relationship with us, it forms the basis for

feeling as if life has no purpose. The truth is our greatest purpose starts and ends on a much greater scale and one of supernatural limitlessness – in God. However, there are many of us who cannot initially see it. We have a tendency to base our entire worth and value on other people; what they say, what they think and what they feel about us as validation of who we are. This is wrong. I believe that our validation is found only in what God says about us which is that we are loved unconditionally, favoured and that each of us have been given the gift of grace through Jesus Christ which allows us to have whatever we want in life. I believe this is what forms the very foundation of who we are.

For some of you reading this story you many not identify with or share my spiritual beliefs, but I guarantee that you will identify with its continued theme on love, relationships, growth and change. We have all been in situations where life has presented us with valley and mountain top moments, so irrespective of our spiritual standing we can identify with each other through similar experiences which see all of us go through the different seasons of life which are ultimately to strengthen and bring us up higher.

My journey of self-discovery and love came at the tender age of fifteen. I had started exploring makeup and trying to find my own sense of style whilst becoming increasingly interested in boys. I came from a traditional West Indian background where boys were not on the agenda (as my mother liked to put it) and my focus was to be on my studies. However, like any teenage girl I was interested in boys and that interest and my first ever "boyfriend" came in the form of my cousin's best friend who was popular and handsome, and who seemed to like me. Our union was not a serious one and didn't last very long but as my first experience of love and rejection, he left an imprint on my heart which began the building blocks of how I viewed my worth and value through emotional connections.

This is what often happens to many of us, particularly young women, where our early experiences of love relationships form the basis of our confidence and how we view ourselves. For me, this was very much the case and having never grown up with my father, I had no real understanding of men or what a good relationship with a man should have been like other than the failed ones I had experienced. I now know that as I grew older I became self-seeking in my quest to better understand men and that came in the form of placing my all into each relationship I encountered. As a result, I became more and more focused on understanding them as opposed to understanding myself and with it I became lost. But then God stepped in and changed my very existence. The moment I realised that I could no longer do things by my own strength changed the dynamics of my life. I went from feeling broken and underserving of love, to a place of being fearless and free. In my understanding what that truly meant required stepping out in faith and believing the truth in the word of God which repeatedly expresses His love for us….His love for me. It meant exploring and believing that I was truly redeemed, beautiful and called personally by God. It meant accepting that nothing could ever separate me from His love if only I would dare to believe in His capabilities over my life.

And that is what happened; I made a choice to believe and trust that through His word, His truth, HIS strength, I am becoming all that I can be and have everything I need to live this life on earth a whole person, accepted and as someone who forms a crucial part in life's journey.

As a woman of God who has lived through loss, I have found something greater than that which I thought I could not survive without and that is through knowing who I am in Christ. Nothing can separate me from His love and with it I have everything. This story has been written to open your hearts and minds to new possibilities and to ignite a greater passion for the life you have been given and a deeper love for the beauty that has been created in you. Let your mind and your heart run free as the words on these pages unfold.

Janine Cummings

CHAPTER 1

Questions

"In the beginning, there was him, and he was the man that was
'Everything'.

In my heart I always believed that somewhere down the long and winding road that was my love affair with him, there would be a stop sign saying it was over and that love no longer lived there anymore. I knew it. Maybe I'd always known it. I could feel it as strongly as the air that I breathed. The relationship would not survive, but I was always hopeful.

I can only describe my love for him as being like the continuation of the ocean and the sky; so intricately intertwined can the two in love appear that it is often difficult to see where one stops and the other begins. This in its entirety was me; this is how I saw 'Everything' and I - as one - one love, one soul, one being - and so I tried to live out every day with a determined spirit.

My love flowed to and through 'Everything' without divide, but somehow I knew that it was not strong enough to carry the relationship to forever on its own as I sensed that deep down inside his own heart he had already decided on its fate.

I would often sit and reflect on the imbalance, looking at him with a sense of gratitude for having what I thought was a wonderful man in my life, but the inexplicable feeling of sadness which accompanied that gratitude haunted me, telling me that it would soon enough be over. It were as though there was a place in his heart where I would never be allowed to go; a place where he was unreachable.

He always seemed to keep me at arm's length, so it was clear to me that I would never make the connection, not fully, and the overwhelming fear of losing him would very often incapacitate me, muddling my thinking and distorting my view of the relationship. I was literally disabled, so to speak. I could neither dismiss nor ignore the nagging persistent feeling that I was not the one for him, and these thoughts began affecting my confidence in the relationship and my behaviour. I began to feel as if I were putting in the work for someone else's gain. That another woman was going to achieve the full potential of his love while I was left with nothing and the saddening, very sobering thoughts, continually pulled apart the foundations of my heart.

This thought pattern continued to disable me and as it did so, it further affected me emotionally. I constantly felt paranoid and continually questioned his actions whenever they appeared to be less than caring towards me. This is when the issue of trust first reared its ugly head. It was disruptive and destructive, and it would prove to be the catalyst for events that culminated in the beginning of the end for me and 'Everything'.

The reality of it all is that each and every one of us, at least once in our lives, will experience the loss of a loved one through a relationship, but we are never quite prepared for that reality or what it can cost us. That loss can feel like a thief in the night, robbing you of what you have always thought of as truth, and in doing so without a hint of pity. It can feel as if it were passing over you taking all that you hold dear firmly gripped in hand, and not looking back for a second. Unfortunately I was met with this at full force, and despite the obvious warning signs of an end drawing near, still, and most ironically, I was not prepared for the inconceivable end which screamed out the inevitable.

The day my world began to fall apart was the 25th of January. I had just moved into a brand new home with my Mr 'Everything' and the future felt bright. Although I had my questions, I had him and that was all that mattered. Comfortably I sat back, arms and legs stretched out on the sofa whilst I watched 'Everything' move around, cooking in the kitchen. I looked at him with adoration as he stood there, cutting up vegetables and preparing a meal for us. He was my hero and my strength. I felt lucky…blessed to have this man in my life because he made me feel complete, and so naturally I wanted more.

It was never intended to be one sided, where I was the only person to gain in the relationship, because I too wanted to give him more and all that I had within me, but in wanting to give him more I felt a desire to believe confidently that 'Everything' was mine and I was his. I wanted to believe that I was his one and only forever love, a love he had expressed to me in the beginning, when he said he felt it was true love – that I was his true love!

I sat there contemplating the idea of when he might be ready to marry me. I was by no means confident of the answer, but I desired to know the truth and so I asked the question. The answer, however, did not meet with my dreams and aspirations, nor did it even reach anywhere near what I had hoped for. The answer was 'no'. He did not want to marry me and neither did he know when - or even if. All that 'Everything' knew confidently and articulated particularly well was the fact that he did not want to have a conversation of this nature at that moment or in a year's time. He did not want to get engaged 'for the sake of it'. He did not feel ready to get married and he was not happy with me or the foundations of the relationship.

Yes, this was the beginning of the end.

So there I was, sitting in what felt like a parallel universe, watching myself, sad and broken-hearted, and being there in that moment hyperconscious of every demoralising word whilst I listened to 'Everything' express how he felt. I stared at him, though he refused to make any eye contact with me. I desperately hoped that if I could just catch a glimpse of his eyes, if I could get him to look at me - really see me - perhaps his heart would soften toward me, but it did not work. He never looked back at me...not once. Instead he stood there and continued to prepare dinner and gesturing with his hands, whilst he said that he could not explain why; he just knew that he did not want to marry me. Those words screamed in my head. He did not want to marry me, but despite being confused as to why not, I had always sensed his truth.

'Everything' rarely raised his voice, but this subject matter seemed to evoke a louder more definitive pitch from him. He didn't shout, but he certainly wanted to be heard. There was no hesitation, no hint of fear or regret. His words were clear. Brokenness overwhelmed me and I felt cold. Numb even. The feeling took my breath away and I could no longer speak. In that moment, it felt as if hours - days even - had passed by. My life had altered in a matter of minutes.

I was confused. Previously marriage had always seemed a clear part of the plan for our future, so what had changed? Was it me or was it him? Or was it just us? Was it just that we no longer worked anymore?

As I sat there, I continued to look at him in disbelief. A growing sense of upset began turning into anger, and despite my growing resentment, I began wishing I could take back my question. That big question had generated an even bigger response, but one I was not prepared for. By now it was also evident to me that I wasn't prepared for things to unfold like this, in what felt as such an emotionally brutal way. I felt as though my heart had been beaten without mercy. My spirit was battered and my emotions were bruised and in turmoil. It was time to wave the white flag. I had lost this round and I knew it, but how was I going to recover from this?

Perhaps if I just screamed out "I was wrong to ask you", it would all just go away, but there was something inside me that stopped that action, as if there were a gag over my mouth forcing the words back down deep within. This really had gone too far, but it was too late. I continued to listen but could no longer look at him. I had to carry on. Perhaps I'd lost the battle, but maybe not the war.

I had to find out the truth; did he love me or not? I took a deep breath and exhaled, preparing myself to say what had to be said. I didn't want to ask. I didn't want to speak. I wanted to hide and live to fight another day. I wanted to bite back my words, turn back the clock, rewind.

My heart began to race, with increasing adrenalin pumping through my body. I could feel it all bubbling up. My breathing became heavier and it was evident in my voice as I began expressing the real truth of how I was feeling. This was something I had previously been unable to do because of my fear of losing

'Everything'. I was nervous because I knew at this point there really was no going back, but felt that I had to be completely honest and true with him about the desires of my heart. I wanted to see our relationship move forward. After all, I loved 'Everything'.

In my heart, I had made a choice to be with him forever, but that decision did not happen overnight nor was it a flippant idea or passing phase. The love I felt was based on a promise we had made to each other from the very beginning. I believed in what he had shown me and what I had shown him.

I remember 'Everything' telling me earlier on in our relationship that he had made a choice to love me and that it had 'always been me'.

So there I was, sat in a completely contradictory scenario watching him go back and forth whilst he talked over what was clearly an uncomfortable subject for him, but one that he was sure of. My heart went from a quick pace to a slowly sinking sensation. I felt as if a bomb had gone off in my head and all that remained was pressure. It hurt. I did not want to let go. I did not want to tell him it was over. All I could do was try to make sense of the chaos I was feeling. I tried to shift the pressure in my mind. I had to. If he didn't want to marry me, if he didn't see a point to it, then it was over. And so it was. I broke up with him that very same night. Neither he nor I tried to talk each other round. We simply went our respective ways, each to the opposite end of the small apartment which was supposed to be our home together, but now it felt further from a home of any sort. It just felt fragmented, damaged and destroyed.

After he went to bed, I sat up and I cried. I cried not only because it was over, but because this brand new home was supposed to be a fresh start and a place of further commitment in taking our relationship forward…or so I had thought. I sat there alone knowing that the future was uncertain. I sat there feeling lost. I sat there feeling as if God had forsaken me because I had allowed myself to lose my way.

I realised all this was happening because I had tried to circumvent God's control in my relationship with 'Everything' by doing things of my own will – not by His. God, who should have been the very foundation of our relationship, had mistakenly been taken out of the process of leading it in the right direction. As a result, I felt as if God's love was gone and I sat there in complete turmoil, not knowing what to do.

Next door in the bedroom, 'Everything' was asleep, and whilst I pondered what my next step should be, I still hadn't grasped the reality that, as far as this relationship was concerned, there really wasn't much else I could do at this point. Neither resources nor the strength was available to fix this mess, and it was at this time that I should have called out to God but I did not.

What was my next move on the Chess Board of Life? How could I turn this back around? How could I fix it all? What was I going to do?! Questions kept circling my mind over and over like a Ferris wheel, but still I had no answers. There was no light bulb moment, there was no hint from my womanly intuition and there was certainly no revelation from God; just the silence of my fears. These thoughts became overwhelming and I began to panic.

All I kept thinking was "you've messed up" as I turned and looked toward the bedroom where 'Everything' was. I got up and walked over to the bedroom door. Quietly I turned the handle, opened it softly and poked my head through the tiny gap between the frame to see if he was still awake, but he wasn't. He was fast asleep, looking peaceful and content. I wanted to just cuddle up next to him and whisper in his ear that it was okay; that it didn't matter if he didn't want to marry me and that I loved him just the same. But something stopped me. I knew that a boundary had been crossed in our relationship and we could never go back. I felt I just couldn't live. What had changed that night was the very thing that stopped me from reaching out to 'Everything' in that very moment. So instead I squeezed my eyes shut and gently closed the door so as to not wake him. I returned and sat back down on the very same sofa which I had comfortably stretched out on earlier that evening before this had all begun and cried.

In that very moment of my sadness, I tried to pray and seek God for comfort, but my mind was distracted and the words would not pass my lips. I could not call to My Father. In desperation, I squeezed my eyelids shut even tighter than before, as I tried harder to pray out my emotions, but I could not focus enough to visualise

His light. I just could not find it. Every thought was clouded and the more I fought to find my way spiritually, the more I felt lost and my thoughts fell into hopelessness. I was numb. I kept visualising myself out in the middle of the ocean treading water, but then panicking as I realised the depth of it. I had lost my ability to stay afloat and I began sinking; drowning in fact. I paused there in that feeling for what felt like hours until I fell asleep in my tears.

In the days following the breakup, I went along acting as if I weren't affected. I carried on for weeks pretending as if it didn't matter to me and that really, I was okay – good in fact. I continued pretending as if I didn't care and that I was relieved to be free of the burden when deep down I was mourning the loss of my love daily. There was a part of me which had decided that I wouldn't give up on him. To me, this man 'Everything' was worth fighting for because from the very beginning I had laid the foundations of a promise. Even when 'Everything' expressed his boredom and lack of interest in me – not so much by his words but by his actions - I would not fully let him go because I had committed to love him regardless. It did not matter who he was. It did not matter what he did or didn't do, or what mood he was in; I loved him. I chose to love him. So the promise would remain even in what appeared to be complete darkness. It was a move of faith and the substance of hope which I held for the future.

I firmly believe that God has a plan for us all and that plan includes an unconditional love that is not based solely on our circumstances, but is a love that is given freely and by choice. I had always thought that, through the many tests and trials of everyday life, God would teach each of us what it truly means to make a choice to love a man or a woman on purpose even when we do not feel like it. I always believed my love for 'Everything' and his love for me was the kind of love that would stand the test of time; one that I was lucky enough to have received. However, I found myself in a scenario where this was clearly not the case, even though I once believed it was.

I would often reflect on these thoughts during long runs, when I needed to clear my head and find clarity. I would weigh up what had been promised with what I felt, and convince myself that there was something still there to fight for. I needed to hold on to something during the initial days of the break up that would guide me on and give me the strength to survive the fallout.

I knew that there was no easy answer – both 'Everything' and I had been hurt and were not only lost in our relationship, we were lost to each other. To a great degree, we had also lost our way with God. After fighting a long battle with my feelings of fear and insecurity over what to do, I made a choice to love 'Everything' even in the hard times. Even when I didn't like him, I loved him. Even when I felt as if I were dying inside from the rejection and ignorance, still I would love him. When I felt confused by his cold and harsh reactions, I would suck it up, take a deep breath and press on. Even when his barrier went up and he would say "no", I would still stretch out my arms. It was unconditional love. I knew that I was no angel and that I myself held some responsibility for the breakdown in our relationship, but I was willing to work at it and try if he would only let me. As I continued on in my thoughts during long runs, I would reflect back on the night I asked that dreaded question of when he would commit to me with marriage, and wished deeply that I had not said a word.

In life, we should never ask a question if we are not truly prepared for the answer, any answer, especially the one we may not want to hear. In this case, I felt that it had not been worth the outcome of events, and things would have been very different had I not opened my big mouth. I felt it was my fault. I felt frustrated, in part, over my continuous need to control our relationship and to have all things play out to my exact timing. At that moment I felt as if it were all down to my unreasonable behaviour, lack of patience and lack of trust in God's timing. This was the cause of all the hurt and pain, and for what?

Despite my regrets, the love was disappearing. It had already begun to shift. The habit was still there, but the love was definitely changing rapidly and not for the better. In me the love began to transform, but it never left, whilst the love in 'Everything', if it were really ever there at all, began to leave. The more separate we were - sleeping in separate rooms, little to no hugs and kisses - the more separate our emotions became. In my heart, I never left 'Everything' but 'Everything' left me.

At this stage I believed that he may have felt as if there was something missing in his life and by now it was a void I could no longer fill. Perhaps our relationship was all too much too soon? 'Everything' and I had experienced an unexpected closeness early on in our relationship that some might say was too close. We were inseparable in a matter of months, and moved in together in the first year of our relationship. It was all very grown up from the get-go and hinted at a "forever" status with the many plans we had both discussed. In hindsight, I could see how that was a recipe for failure, but I was in the moment and I was in love.

The reality, upon reflection, is that 'Everything' and I couldn't sustain what we had at first promised because the love between us was different now. I also believe that if God is not always a firm part of the plan, then there is nothing you can do to make it succeed. I guess it can for a time, but it will never have longevity. You see, as soon as 'Everything' and I took God out of the equation, the love was gone from our relationship. Habit remained, yes, but the love not so much.

I paused further for thought and remembered one of the first things that Mr 'Everything' had said to me when we had met. He said that he prayed to God for his wife and that he had prayed specifically for that person to have certain qualities. Soon after, he met me and I seemed to match what he wanted. I couldn't help but wonder what may have changed, and more importantly, what went wrong? I later came to believe that I never did, nor would I ever, fit the brief. I was too different to what 'Everything' was used to, but at the time I questioned it over and over again, asking God why. I wanted to know what I could do, and I was determined to work it out in order to fix things. So I thought back, further delving into the memory files, searching for more clues and answers. At this point, trying to find answers was all that I had and my only way to survive.

CHAPTER 2

Reflection

It's always easy and beautiful in the beginning of a new relationship. A new relationship will often be filled with good feelings and optimism. The truth is that as a relationship grows in familiarity, it gets harder and those warm, fuzzy feelings begin to fade as they are replaced by a choice to love. When I reflected on the relationship, I searched for what went wrong in the massive memory vault of my mind. I was extremely hard on myself and I believed that it was my failure in the relationship that caused it to end. I would blame myself over and over again, torturing my mind as I insisted on dissecting every intricate detail. I would review the many months and years, replaying different events over the time of my relationship with 'Everything', trying to find clues and obvious indicators that had led to its demise. I believed that in doing so, somehow I could rescue it. Each week I would go out on lengthy runs in an attempt to clear my mind, so that hopefully I could extract the vital clues which would release me enough to escape my pain and allow me to find a moment of peace. It allowed me to think clearly, but during those runs where I would hit long distances, replacing the pain of my mind with pain in my body, it became very difficult to make conclusive sense of anything. I would often return home, legs barely able to move and my body trembling from the adrenalin but nothing ever profound or resolute sprung from the haze in my mind. Naively, each and every time, I looked forward to a revelation or a real sense of peace, but I received nothing new – just a raw feeling of being back to square one.

Home was supposed to be where my heart was, but our home was filled only with sadness and so my injured heart felt further away from that secure feeling. There was complete separation in how we lived and often conversations were only in passing. It all felt platonic and clinical and I hated it. I felt cheated and could not understand why God had allowed this crash to happen causing our relationship to fall apart. At the time I didn't feel as if I was blaming God as such, but I regularly questioned why He had not rescued us….rescued me. It made no sense at all as I had always strongly believed that essentially we had both tried to live by what were God's standards on the limited resources afforded to us, and so in my mind I felt that surely God would have given credit for our efforts, but there was seemingly no credit given and no rescue. I remained confused and overwhelmed which only pushed me further away from God as I battled against believing I was being punished. It didn't help with the fact that I had recently left my old church and was not plugged in to a new one, so the essential spiritual fuel I needed was running on empty. I was drained and not strong enough to fight off all those negative thoughts and feelings that were not of God. The enemy foothold had begun to take place and as my doubts and fears grew even stronger; my connection with God grew weaker. In my sadness and dejection my voice became quiet and my prayer life suddenly became sporadic to non-existent. I could feel my spirit growing weaker as the battle continued on. I was continually torn between various conflicting emotions which would flurry from peace to rage, to fear and resentment, then a feeling of paranoia and guilt. It literally destroyed me. Usually, during such times of spiritual struggle, I had always been able to turn to my mentor and best friend 'Everything'. He would always know what to do and would give me the wisdom to see a way out of struggle and always had the words to calm me, but because we were no longer together I could not turn to him. I was alone. Unable to cope without him, I turned to close friends and would talk with them for hours about how I felt, what I was going through and what I felt 'Everything' was doing to me, forgetting what he might have been going through himself. I would ask for answers from friends to help determine what I should do in a hope that they could help, but instead I became the biggest gossip in my own situation as I repeated the same things over and over again. I felt trapped in a vicious cycle which despite wanting to get out of, I couldn't. It only served to be disruptive as I became weighed down by the opinions of others in addition to what I thought was my own conclusive understanding. Never once did I turn to God for counsel. After all, I had concluded that God was punishing me and had left me to go it alone, so how could I turn to Him? I listed a multitude of reasons why I couldn't turn to God and the enemy convinced me of so many things that were untrue; that God didn't love me, that nothing I did would work out and that it was impossible to recover from the disappointment and loss. It all drove me further away from My Father as I felt angry towards Him and then guilty for blaming Him for my own mistakes, but the feelings kept me in place of shame and so I remained determined to go it alone even though being alone was not where I truly wanted to be. I hated feeling out in the wilderness – it was confusing and uncomfortable, but I truly did not know a way out. I began to feel lonely again in the same way I had felt in my life before meeting 'Everything' and it caused my mind to descend into chaos.

The months following the night of the question were extremely difficult ones for both myself and 'Everything'. We tried to be somewhat kind and amicable to each other enough so that we could get along – after all we still had to live together until the end of our contract, but we had struggled and the more we tried, the greater the struggle became. Individually we were both under pressure and that pressure made us act in ways that were less than fruitful. For me I found that I needed to focus…refocus, but all I did was find various methods of distractions and none of which worked. Initially I had tried to be on my best behaviour and act in a way which I thought would win favour with 'Everything' but when my efforts were not acknowledged by him I looked for alternative attention and began talking to another man. I had not intended to do anything but I needed some kind of distraction in order to feel better about myself, especially when it dawned on me that 'Everything' seemed distracted by another woman himself. Just knowing that another woman could make him smile as if he didn't have a care in the world was a sobering reality of the impending change I was fighting against, so in an effort to wipe out any additional pain I began talking to a man from my past. Although it did not go beyond talks on the phone and there was some degree of intention, I was never brave enough to take it any further nor did I really want to. Every time the other man suggested meeting up I would find an excuse not to go. Nevertheless, I did enjoy our conversations as they helped with my grief but our interactions did not last long as I began to feel guilty. I thought about 'Everything' and how he might feel had he known what I was doing. Deep down in my heart I knew that I didn't really want anything to happen with the man from my past because I was still in love with the man from my present even if we weren't together. Soon enough the phone calls slowed down grinding to a halt as the man from my past began to lose interest caused by my continuous excuses and avoidance each time he suggested we meet up. Before long I was back to being alone, lying awake at night thinking about 'Everything' whilst he lay asleep in the room next door. All I could think about was my love and the current status of our relationship. We were still separated and it was obvious that reconciliation was not on the cards. Even though 'Everything' had seemed to be temporarily distracted by another woman, he saw the error of his ways and admitted he still loved me. However, it was clear that he still needed some time alone to get himself back on the right track and reconnect with God. Whilst I felt a sense of relief in knowing that whoever 'she' was, was no longer in the picture, I still felt intimidated by the fact that his focus was solely on God and I was not even the smallest of factors. I didn't understand it and questioned his logic over loving me but not wanting to be with me. If he still cared for me in a romantic way and wanted to be the best he could be for me in the future, why were we not working on getting right with God together? Whilst there was a claim of some love, we were still so very separate and it killed me to know that he didn't want me in his life at that time. I had spent two plus years of my life focusing on 'Everything'...all his needs, all his desires and all his wants, but there was no return of focus from him onto me. I had always wanted to make him happy as his happiness was my happiness but in searching for the way to effectively do that, I never consulted with God or looked to Him for answers in trying to gain some kind of perspective. It felt all too much like hard work trying to focus on God when all I wanted to do was just have 'Everything' back.

I dug myself deeper into a pit of despair as I continued to ignore God by trying to figure out my own resolution to what it was that I needed to do to make it all right and to fix all the things wrong in my broken relationship with 'Everything'. The problem was that the more I dug my heels in ignoring God and trying to go it alone, the more insecure I would feel, especially as 'Everything' made it clear that he was not interested in any form of romantic reconciliation with me at that time and this left me feeling even more insecure and rejected. It was then that I began to invade his privacy by checking up on him as I was convinced there had to be more to his lack of interest in me. Whilst I knew that I had probably reacted in a similar way to most given the situation, it was wrong and definitely not the answer. I realised that my actions only led to more insecurity and distrust on both sides as it became obvious I was checking up on him. 'Everything' would either catch me out or I would blurt out my findings in a fit of anger as I confronted him with proof and confirmation of what I saw as his unfaithfulness. Whenever I saw something on Facebook or on his phone that suggested complete conflict with what he had said in relation to loving me, I would unravel as quickly as thread from a falling spindle and with it I would lose a little more perspective each time, as I began disconnecting from any sense of self control. My impetuous behaviour did nothing more than to push 'Everything' even further away and give him another reason as to why we couldn't be together. There was a lack in trust. It was at that point I realised if there was to be any chance of a reconciliation I was preventing it by spoiling the possibility with my own irresponsible and childish behaviour. I knew that I needed to trust him and if I didn't, I at least needed to trust God enough to know confidently that He would work on and lead 'Everything' in the right direction, but I just couldn't bring myself to do it. I felt that I couldn't surrender the situation over to God because the fear of uncertainty overwhelmed my emotions and I became lost and destitute. I reflected over my lack of resources and inability to turn things around and in that moment of reflection, I began to cry. With my head hung low and eyes filled with tears, I realised how much I had missed God my Father, but I deliberated over my rapid decline to think and react logically and concluded that I could not go to Him. How could I go to God in my moment of madness? It felt futile to explore the possibility as I was overridden with guilt and shame. Once again I had abandoned God when things got tough, but even in recognising that I missed Him, I still convinced myself that I could not go to God for help with the burden of 'Everything'. Despite my hesitance, there was still something of a pull inside me that drew me to a place of wanting and a need within to reach out in prayer. I didn't know what to say or how to verbalise the many words that needed to be said out aloud as my breath felt weak, but I had just enough inside of me to utter the words "Father God, please help me". Despite expressing the words calling on God, the atmosphere remained silent and I struggled to feel any connection with The Father. I sat back in quiet contemplation as I continued on believing that He had either not heard me or was purposely ignoring my cries for help because I struggled to feel even a slight difference and it most certainly felt as if there had been no change.

Still I carried on living a life of loneliness. 'Everything' and I were still separate in the majority of the day to day practises we use to embark upon together, and it became an even greater strain to look at him each and every day, and not be able to reach out to him as I always had done. Conversations were limited and more often than not he barely looked at me. There were times when he would close himself away from me spending time in an alternative room either on his phone or computer game. It felt as if he just wanted to get away from me along with all that reminded him of our failed relationship. I had become a stranger to him; a distant, vague memory in his heart. It was as if I had become a shell of my former self in his eyes and a giant void likened to the black hole – vast and empty. Although I was hurt by the idea that he no longer felt any connection to me, I never believed for a moment that his actions were deliberate or that 'Everything' intended to hurt or to mistreat me as it seemed as if he too were going through what I thought was some kind of trauma and pain. I interpreted his behaviour as a coping method for dealing with the changes even though there were times when it was hard to accept the transition. There was also a part of me that had to accept and suck it all up because I had been the person who initially ended it all by telling 'Everything' it was over for good. As a result, I could only assume that 'Everything' was responding to his sadness in the only way he knew how. However, I recognised a distinctive change. Yes there was a definite sadness, but there was also some anger and a real sense of tiredness about him which made 'Everything' seemingly give up on wanting to meet anyone's expectations anymore, especially mine.

We spent a number of months trying to live at first as amicable acquaintances, quickly followed up with trying to be so-called friends. It was the only way forward to try and survive the wilderness, but there was a continual rapid decline. The first time it really hit me that we were no longer romantically linked and only in the friend zone was when I found out that he had changed my contact name in his phone. 'Everything' had always listed me as 'Da Wife' but instead he had changed my profile back to what felt like my less significant government name. I was no longer that special person and the one who stood out among the rest, not only on his phone display but it his heart. I was downgraded and I felt hugely insignificant. The initial shock took my breath away as I wasn't sure how to feel, and as I digested the reality of another uncomfortable change a tear fell from my eyes. On reflection, it was this moment that I realised his intentions were set and his decision about my future in his life were final. The blow left me feeling winded as I struggled to breathe. I had not even thought about the possibility of no longer being that person to him, but now the ugly truth was staring me in the face. When I questioned him over his decision to downgrade my status, he explained his reasoning were to do with intention and speaking things into being. Whilst I accepted it without fuss inside I was devastated and it became clear that his actions meant the prospect of reconciliation was fading further away and into the deep. He no longer saw me as that person; she was someone else and I felt that it was finally confirmed I had been side stepped to make way for the real and future wife. In that moment I knew he would continue on in his journey to seek out the real love of his life and it wouldn't take long for him to find her. I knew that there were a number of younger women eagerly waiting to take my place and happy to, and there would be nothing I could do to stop it. Again I felt angry at my situation, but then I became even angrier at myself. After all, it was me who had caused him to take affirmative action in moving on as a result of forcing things on him he wasn't yet ready for. More to the point, rather than seeing it all for what it was by accepting that we were both in different places and trusting God through the process, I instead projected my residual anger onto others. The growing tension in my mind made me look at everyone with suspicious eyes and I questioned everyone's motives. 'Everything' was at the top of my list of suspects although it made no real sense. We were no longer together nor each other's responsibility but somehow I could not correlate that reality with my emotions. I still felt that he owed me some degree of loyalty and explanation for his actions, but in truth he did not and I had no right to expect that of him either. All I could focus on was a feeling of distrust and the repetitive theme ran through my mind of questioning who was going to be the woman to take him away, making him pack his bags and leave our home to start pastures new forever. I couldn't let the thoughts go and in my mind I was determined not to let it happen whilst 'Everything' still remained living in our home and with me. I felt that there was still a chance and I was going to try my hardest at one final shot to bring it all back. The problem was that in addition to my heightened sense of paranoia thinking that everyone had a motive, I no longer trusted 'Everything'. The trust had already begun disappearing long before we had even split up and as a result it felt as if the fractures were so deep they were beyond healing. All I could focus on was the idea that he was in pursuit of happiness elsewhere, readily looking for my replacement, the new "wife" even though I had no real concrete evidence of anything sinister. However, the seeming lack of love and compassion towards me made me feel as if there was a greater conspiracy to find the new "her." I knew that I should have been taking these difficult feelings of insecurity and struggles directly to God through prayer and petition, but I did not. I did what was familiar and returned to my go to methodology, by consulting my mind and turning things over and over again until it became so painful I didn't know what to do with it. I felt grieved, and because I was consumed by my own feelings I projected it on to 'Everything' and became unkind to him. I was snappy, argumentative and debateable, and I continued to question all of his actions which made my insecurities force me to become the very person I had never wanted to be in his life. I had become that person who left him because he no longer fitted with my plans. I had become the person who walked away when he may have still needed me, and I had become the person who said he was not good enough just as he was. On further reflection, I realised that through our relationship I had never given him the chance to grow into the man he needed to become in Christ among other things. I was too impetuous. I had been misguided by my own belief system, thinking that my opinion was the only one that mattered in my relationship with 'Everything', but it was only that - an opinion; there were times when that opinion was proven wrong, as I later learned when the consequences of an opinion changed my life for good. In my mind our relationship should have followed a particular chronological pattern in its life cycle, but when too much time had begun to elapse without the necessary progress, I believed something needing fixing and more often than not it was him. It was evident that in places my relationship with 'Everything' had developed on my timing and by my direction and neither by his or God's, but I could not see it at the time. Instead of recognising the revelation and using it to my advantage to help restore us, I became super critical of 'Everything' to the point where nothing he ever did was right. Even the simplest of things were written off as wrong in my book as I grew in resentment during the period of what I viewed as lack of working towards reconciliation. I was resentful because it became increasingly apparent he did not want to take things further, but I believe he too came to know of the resentment I carried inside of me. I believe that even when 'Everything' was trying I never gave him a real chance and I would never give any real credit for very much of what he did. It got to the stage where I could no longer recognise his efforts of love and didn't know how to receive it. I can remember during a brief period of reconciliation following the initial breakup where he would attempt to kiss or cuddle me in a display of affection and I would return his attempt with a frosty reception, questioning his actions instead of simply just accepting the love from him in that moment. Ironically, his actions had always been what I longed for. I had craved it, and prayed earnestly for it (when I had actually been able to pray) but there I stood, not knowing what to with it when faced with his act of kindness. Foolishly my response came in the form of rejection, and I could guess from his reaction that it would be a long time before I would see any kind of attempt to show that he still cared for me in that way again and true to form, that was what happened. No more attempts or displays of affection from 'Everything' and without the guidance from God or leadership from spiritual elders, there seemed nowhere else to go for help. It just became harder and harder and as the weeks then turned into months it were as if we could no longer communicate. We could no longer hear each other and neither did we really want to. Somehow we had both forgotten The Bible's various teachings of being kind to each other, remaining in love with one another by choice and the very prominent teaching of never letting the sun go down over anger. It had all become a distant memory. I knew that I myself had forgotten how to be patient with 'Everything and I most certainly had forgotten any examples of sacrificial love like the love that Christ had demonstrated by dying on the cross for us. We had both forgotten how to love each other with intention and purpose and I knew for myself despite the outcome, I needed to get that back. We had both gone to church as believers in Christ, both studied the bible and spent time in God's presence enough to know what we needed to do, but neither of us were really strong enough at that time and I in particular, failed in any real great strength to push through. I knew on my part that feelings were strongly in control but not ones that identified with walking in God's love. It was a selfish lack of willing to sacrifice some of myself for 'Everything' that left me growing in scarcity. I questioned how two people who had previously declared so much love for one another could find themselves left with jagged edges. We were both in a state of such disconnection and I knew that it had come by straying away from God's purpose in our lives. The division was unrecognisable and far from symbolic of two people who had previously stood firmly together in the very beginning. We had always known and understood the power of Christ's love and the importance of demonstrating it in the past. We had previously understood where we were going spiritually and what we needed to do to survive, but somehow we could no longer demonstrate that love to each other and our survival instincts had gone. It was too painful to watch as I literally saw whatever remained of our relationship die. Our relationship was likened to that of a beautiful flower shedding its petals as it was no longer able to survive by its own strength. I could literally visualise myself frantically trying to restore what was left of the remaining petals that represented us, as they continued to wilt and wither away. We had both tried to water the withering petals of our delicate relationship. We had both tried to salvage what we could, but the shedding of its life seemed beyond our rescue. Each day we would die a little bit more until the final day where there was no more life left in either one of us. Even when it came to that time where the beautiful flower that was our relationship was a distant memory, I still believed that there was a possibility of new life and a hope for the rebirth of something better. I held on to the belief that what seemed to be an end was not as such, because I truly believed and sensed something in my spirit which acted as confirmation that God had brought us together for divine purpose, and was not yet finished with us. The difficulty was that 'Everything' and I were no longer in agreement about our future together and for that reason The Father's purpose could never be realised in both our lives together. For me it was difficult to accept being without 'Everything' nor could I see past the rawness of it all because what should have been so simple instead proved to be more and more difficult. I had always believed that God had a plan which was to see us grow together into fruition but because our own individual plans had changed, the dream became null and void. I knew that God had the ability to move mountains; He could heal my broken heart and allow for the miraculous to happen with 'Everything' and I but we both seemed to lack courage and any real desire to surrender to God's will which would have seen the breakthrough. I realised with a heavy heart that my lack of courage came in the shape of my unstable faith. I continually struggled with believing in God and trusting that He would not see my love fail and that He would do the very best for both of us. In the end that lack of faith cost me the very thing I feared losing, and so when 'Everything' finally packed his bags and left our relationship for good later on that year, I was left holding on to the memories of our past and clinging on to a hope while reflecting on who we once were. In moments of nostalgia I was left wondering why we both just couldn't have held on to those beautiful times we had both created because there were times of real happiness and a small gap of hope where we might have made it to the finish line. I had been so scared to let go because I convinced myself that I would lose 'Everything', but in the end I lost him anyway. Whilst I knew my journey would at some point continue after the pain of his exit had become easier, I knew it was going to have to be a journey without him and that the promise of a future with 'Everything' could no longer remain alive. I knew that in order to move forward I would have to acknowledge that a past I once knew was not reflected in the present, nor could it remain even in a memory. However, and quite often, my memories acted as a comforter and in a brief moment would make me smile. Reflection was and quite literally, the only thing to bring temporary life back to the dry old bones of my emotions before I would return to my sadness. It was the only place I could escape to. It was the

only place I had wanted to be. For in that moment, it was my home.

CHAPTER 3

It Started so Simply

Remaining in a place of my memories, I reminisced over the time I had first met 'Everything'. I reflected on where I had been in my life before he plucked me from obscurity, drawing me in to the hopes of a new life and future. His entrance into my life came at a time when I had no expectation of romance being a potential forecast in my future, but a chance of romance seemed to find me through him. It came at a point when I had given up on any hope of finding love because it felt as if love was not a word in the vocabulary of my existence. It had always been a struggle to find someone who was consistent and intentional and I was worn out by the many failed relationships I had experienced. I often spent time looking at other couples and smile in admiration but my smiles and tender hearted spirit were often followed up with sadness as I could never visualise myself as ever being part of a twosome, or having what others seemed to have. I had completely given up. I believed that love was out of my reach and that I was destined to be alone but when he came into my life that all seemed to change at the drop of a hat. The sudden shift in what seemed to be a dead issue came with surprise and with much confusion but despite it all I developed a growing excitement over the apparent new chapter in my life.

I had met 'Everything' at my local gym during the early part of spring. I was not yet a fitness instructor but was very into exercise and in particular, high intensity training. Our meeting seemed to mark a significant change in season, not only in the weather, but also in my heart and mind. At first I barely even noticed him. I was not interested in very much other than lifting those weights on the gym floor and pushing my body as hard as I could in Boxing and Circuit classes. However, eventually I slowed my pace moving between classes, lifted my head and focused my eyes long enough to look at him, I finally noticed 'Everything' clearly for the first time. His entrance into my life came during a period of chaos where my very existence felt as if it were one of continuous struggle filled with emotional challenges. My life had only been survival and not really the life God had wanted me to always have. I had fallen into bad habits which meant I lacked any form of real consistency, direction or drive on a day to day basis. The heavy load of the life I led often meant that I was left feeling burdened but with his arrival, 'Everything' seemed to lighten the load. From the very beginning he acted as a bright light in my darkness, and with it my confidence began to grow. I began to believe that perhaps we had crossed paths with divine timing and that God had actually sent him into my life with a purpose. For a long time I had struggled with the ever growing problems presented before me and a multitude of complex issues which included family feuds, fighting with my own sense of low self-esteem, lack of self-love and the most important of all, a lack in any real relationship with God. I had felt as if my life were spiralling out of control and it seemed to reveal very little to look forward to…but then there was something else and that something was effortless and good. It was 'Everything'. His presence seemed to speak life into being and with it came an instant shift in my attitude which encouraged me to sit up and take notice of him. It all came unexpectedly, but there was a welcomed change that took place within me which was influenced by his presence. My life began to take on a whole new meaning. He was a dominant force and one I had not anticipated nor was truly ready for.

'Everything' was truly a breath of fresh air, but once I admitted to myself that I actually liked him, I went to work on trying to ignore the newly developing feelings. I started off by convincing myself that I couldn't possibly be attracted to him and justified the emotions as unrealistic. I rationalised the exploration

of new emotions down to loneliness, fear and a feeling of panic
brought on by the idea of being a certain age and still single, but
despite my efforts I couldn't deny his ever growing presence in my
heart. I knew very little about who he was but knew just enough
to confirm I wanted him in my life; however, I was unsure of how
and in what capacity. I couldn't figure that out. I continued on
with a number of discussion points in my mind but came to no
resolve. I questioned what 'Everything' might have been thinking
considering someone like me, but then laughed off any idea of
him really being attracted to me in a romantic sense. It was futile
to think that it was at all possible but still there was definitely
something there. I felt somewhat encouraged in my soul to visualise
and step into a place that felt comfortable and encouraging; a place
where there was assurance in a feeling of trust, but with it all came
a feeling of great fear. Not knowing which way to go, I struggled
with understanding what was happening within me or why I felt so
drawn to a man who seemed to go against all the odds but feelings
began growing with intensity. In an attempt to come to some sort
of conclusion, I weighed up the trust with the fear. The feeling of
trust came owing to what was a seemingly honest way about him.
'Everything' was the epitome of integrity as he was intentional in
what he said, his actions mirrored his intentions, and he had a
great deal of compassion for those he cared about. He stood at 6ft
3" tall and although more often than not held a serious expression
which made him seem unapproachable; he was a kind hearted man
and a gentle giant. The contrast was all the more attractive to me

especially when he expressed a love for his grandmother who he talked about with great passion and referred to as his best friend. He inspired my very being. He had a walk and a way about him that was relaxed and carefree and his presence in my life became very warming. It felt good to me. Even watching him at a distance I felt alive in his presence and the sheer magnitude of his very being was explosive. It would cause my heartbeat to quicken as an overwhelming shyness would take hold within me just at the very thought of him. It felt as if 'Everything' was my rainbow after a big storm and despite the fear caused by a lack of understanding, I looked to him with anticipation.

On reflection, I could not pinpoint when it was or how our initial conversation happened, but when we spoke for the first time the very words shared between us lead to the start of it all. It was so easy with 'Everything' and he made me feel comfortable in his presence. We would talk for long periods of time but often our conversations felt as if they were too short, passing by within minutes, seconds even. 'Everything' was not a big talker as such but he was wise in his words and he would listen carefully to all that I had to say, responding with the right advice or knowledge in a subject matter. Often I tried to keep my cool by not revealing too much interest in our deeper conversations which mostly centred around Christianity and whilst I would never confirm any real acknowledgement, inside I felt deeply moved by our time in talks together. I would often find myself feeling as if our conversations were too short and with each one passing a growing lack in fulfilment and a greater longing for more. Our time would always feel so precious to me and the value of that time was ever increasing. I can remember there being moments of dispute within my own family where I would feel deeply saddened by a volatile situation, but 'Everything' would be there with me on the other end of the phone, listening and encouraging me through. He was a constant support and comfort and a great source of recovery and strength. It was impossible to ignore such a kind heart which was seemingly so selfless. I wouldn't have said it was love at that point, but he had a truly intentional way about him that was a gift from the Holy Spirit and that gifting was used to love and care for the weak. It felt, very deeply, as if God was using him to reach me on a deeper level.

'Everything' would often talk about Christ, sending me scriptures and quotations from The Bible in an effort to further encourage me. He would speak with such a passionate love for Jesus and an ever tenderness towards God which although seemed so simply put, was always so eloquent at the same time. Despite my initial lack of understanding or any real in-depth interest in building a relationship with God through Christ, I felt compelled to listen and hear more. Despite trying to fight my ever gravitating interest to know more and often with a multitude of questions and conflicting spiritual viewpoints to that of 'Everything', I could not ignore his voice for very long no matter how hard I tried. I could not then explain what it was that kept me intrigued or if it was even an increasing desire to understand what it truly meant to be in Christ, but what I did know was that I certainly wanted more and could not stay away from him. I looked forward to our spiritual debates where I continued to challenge 'Everything' and true to form he would always have an answer. I loved it and simply adored our conversations, which lead to adoring him all the more. I continued to crave our interactions as time went on because it always meant that I was able to spend even more time with him. The loneliness I had once felt seemed to disappear and was now replaced with genuine companionship, but the doubtfulness in my nature lead only to confusion and a questioning of its authenticity. I would often question myself somewhat perplexed as to what in particular it was about 'Everything' which made me like him so much. I simply could not identify the source of what was continually drawing me nearer to him especially as we were both so different. He was a Born Again Christian, I wasn't. He was also younger than me and the reality of these differences screamed out a long list of reasons as to why I should keep my distance from. Still I could not stay away. When I questioned myself again over my desire to know more about 'Everything' and to seek more of him, I asked if it were because of the physical attraction or because of a possible sexual desire for him - after all he was what I saw as a handsome man, but it was neither of those things. I came to know and accept that the only source of the attraction to 'Everything' came from God. It was the Holy Spirit working within him that was the guiding light and happiness I found in what he seemed to exude. Just to be near him, to know him and to be with him was a desire for something more than just longing for a man; it was a supernatural connection which came from the hand of the most high. During the initial stages of our relationship, he quickly became my rock of salvation and saving grace. Finding 'Everything' was finding my way to God through the love of Christ which he guided me towards step by step in a gentle, nurturing way. The sad thing about it at the time was that I did not know God was the source of all things concerning our connection because all I could focus my attention on was 'Everything' the man and not 'Everything' My Father, the Almighty.

I always knew that I lacked something in my life but I had not realised that in actual fact it was a lack in a spiritual walk with God. Before I had met 'Everything' and for some considerable time after, whilst I tried to adjust to a new way of doing things, I seemed to continually and quite systematically make decisions in my life filled with bad choices and those that weren't for my greater good. I still had a bad attitude towards those issues centred around relationships and in particular, those with men. As a child and teenager I had experienced various father figures but never formed any real valuable bonds with these men that would encourage healthy relationships in my adult life. Prior to meeting 'Everything' I had a distinct inability to see my worth and value unless I was involved in one way or another with a man often in an unloving relationship and I would crave attention from the kind of men that only wanted one thing from me – sex, never a relationship. However 'Everything' seemed different. He did not pursue me or seem to want to sleep with me from the outset like other men from my past. He seemed built with a genuine interest in my salvation, and so encouraged me to do and be better. It almost felt as if 'Everything' had made it his personal mission with great determination to make my life better which made me feel privileged but even more so, special. Each night during our phone calls, he would leave me with a thought or word which I would be able to draw comfort from. I continued to be pleasantly surprised by his wisdom, and there were times when I would sit back in awe of him because what he represented was in total conflict with my perception of who I thought he should be.

Despite the growing fondness, I still found myself continually wrestling with my conscience over the seemingly obvious challenges that needed to be addressed. It constantly played on my mind that because 'Everything' was younger than I was the age difference alone would be enough of a problem to make any union between us null and void. I questioned what younger man would be able to offer a woman like me, in her thirties with a number of issues, a future and challenged the reasons why he would really want to? I debated if he would truly be able to sustain a committed relationship with me over time and if a relationship with him would be realistic? I continued to wrestle with these feelings and started to doubt his intentions and suitability. I began to see the idea of a genuine relationship with him as a lost cause. I convinced myself because he was younger, his life experience was limited. I felt that I may have been walking into certain failure because eventually he might develop a desire to see if the grass was greener elsewhere and so that too would snatch away from his credibility. I carried on in this manner in what I can only describe as battling with my mind to the point of exhaustion but I always came back to the same conclusion. Despite the differences, 'Everything' was something new and exciting which I had not experienced before and despite the mental notepad of all the "do's and don'ts", I could no longer refute the efforts of a man with such integrity.

As the weeks went by I felt myself becoming increasingly attached to 'Everything' in my developing relationship with him but I continued with my mental debate anguishing over what to with my growing feelings. I toyed with the idea of making a definitive choice to stay away from him, ending all contact immediately in an effort to eradicate the differences which would never go away just because I wanted them to. As a result, it left me feeling somewhat unsure at times of how I should behave towards him but despite the ever growing mixed emotions, I knew there was something that I wanted to explore. I continued to wrestle with my emotions, but with time I saw our union blossom into a relationship and from that developed something I had found difficult to explain or verbalise. It was a very evident type of kinship; a close bond which

I felt was immeasurably special. I didn't fully understand what was happening to me or why my emotional attachment was developing so quickly, but it happened at full force. I didn't feel in control of my emotions and it made me act in panic. As a result, I would subconsciously try to sabotage the growing relationship to cover over my fears. I tried to expose myself to him as someone who was extremely sinful and that our involvement could only seek to cause conflict of interest. I would openly tell him with great confidence that I was the type of person who had no issue with pre-marital sex, almost as if I were goading him into a reaction by my distasteful bragging. I would tell him, quite poker-faced, that I loved it and felt comfortable indulging my flesh in the hope that exposing my flaws would leave him with no illusions over who I was. It was almost as if I was testing him to see if he would react to my powerful and somewhat unsavoury revelations by leaving instantaneously, and prove me right over my fears. So I continued to lay it on the line, telling him that as he was a man of spirit and I was clearly a woman of flesh, we were just too opposite for anything to ever really work out between us. I knew that in truth I never really wanted 'Everything' to leave, but I desperately needed to be sure of his intentions towards me. I believed that if he, as a man of God, could still want to know someone who was so lost even after confessing a spiritual ugliness, then it would prove he was genuinely sincere over his intentions towards me, and act as confirmation that our union was meant to be, and so it was - 'Everything' never left. He was neither deterred nor dissuaded by my shock tactics. If anything he dug deeper, and from that I was able to feel secure. Even in those early days, I felt his love and kindness towards me even though I had done nothing to deserve it. I felt as if he had held out his arms metaphorically speaking, to accept my unclean soul and I felt safe in them. It was then that I knew 'Everything' was the one to make me lose it all and that our union was the start of a new chapter in my life. I felt loved, I felt accepted and I felt it unconditionally even though I continued to battle with my flesh and spirit.

CHAPTER 4

Flesh Versus Spirit

Living a life where you have little to no direction is the foundation
for feeling spiritually void. During the most part of my adult life
and before my relationship with 'Everything' that was me on a
day to day basis: stuck and unable to move forward. As clichéd as
it sounds, I chose to remain at an all too familiar crossroad of the
flesh (as I thought of it) where I often felt perplexed at the thought
of taking any step resulting in taking some sort of definitive action
rather than just hiding away. At times I felt such pain in my mind
that it often was so powerful it seemed to transfix my body. In
response to the difficult emotions and as a means of escape, I would
distract myself with various destructive behaviours choosing only
to walk along a road which carried me to an all too familiar place of

short term gratification. This behaviour allowed me to disassociate myself from taking any real ownership or accountability over my life; it left me not having to deal with the real me or the growing number of people who seemingly hurt me. It was a place where I could get lost in the comfort of my own sin and in the ever growing response to the darkness which continued to build up inside. I developed a deep sense of self-loathing. I began to despise myself greatly for the inability to respond to life more positively. Life itself felt far too difficult to handle other than seeing it and myself as a failure. It was easier to remain feeling defeated and lost in my own pain rather than confront the many demons that plagued me. Dealing with it all was just too much for me to handle and I simply could not accept the work required, which would have led me on a beneficial path to emotional freedom, if only I were to address it all. Instead I hid beneath the surface of burden and remained confined to my mental chains.

I couldn't begin to look at myself as God had always seen me, with love. It was the complete opposite. I convinced myself that I was ugly, unworthy, useless and a loser, in a way to justify the reasoning for what felt like such a destitute and empty life. I felt challenged and really put out by having to deal with the real me each day – someone who I did not like particularly all that much, but had no way to escape from. There were times when I would look at myself in the mirror and cry disappointed with my life. I would look at my body, certain aspects and characteristics in my features and wonder why God had punished me unlike friends and other acquaintances who seemed to have received God's blessing without question. I then questioned why God had given me a life which was so limited and as I continued seeing myself as physically unattractive; the viewpoint transcended to the very corners of my entire being. I did not have time for God as I questioned who He was in my life. It seemed that God had forgotten me when He wrote The Book of Life and although I had always known God through my Christian Catholic faith, I had never had a real relationship with Him. I rarely followed in any routine which included God in my life and only saw Him as a faint authority figure in place to give people some kind of hope and direction in life. I did not view Him with any real substance or have faith in who He was, nor did I care to learn more about what His son Jesus Christ had apparently done to save my life. I refused to allow myself to believe in His so-called capabilities because they seemed impossible. It was also difficult for me to want to know God when I blamed him for so much. I understood that He was the supposed author and finisher of all things, and would make good on His promises for those who believed in and loved Him, but that was not me. It felt unrealistic to place all my hope in something or someone who apparently existed but was never tangible. Nonetheless, there were moments when in great difficulty and often through sheer desperation I would reach out in prayer, often begging for mercy or release from my suffering, but it seemed as though God had never heard me. In the deafening silence of no reply it acted as confirmation that I was truly alone. I felt that I would have to work it all out for myself and map out my own destiny. I was angry, and in my hopelessness I responded with questioning and then determining that there was no point to any belief system. I rationalised that if God wasn't going to acknowledge my lowly existence even through my cries for help, then I would find that "help" elsewhere.

On reflection, I spent much of my early twenties trying to seek comfort in something one way or another once I decided that God was not an option of rescue. Somewhere along the line I developed a growing lack of confidence in the way I looked and was very uncomfortable in my own skin. This insecurity had a tendency to increase after an episode of emotional trauma usually in the form of rejection by a person or persons. In response to my growing anxieties over my appearance, I spent a lot of time and money trying to alter my looks as best I knew how with the limited resources available. As part of my daily routine each and every morning, I would allow for a lengthy designated amount of time to apply makeup. It would take hours as I put on large amounts of various cosmetics in a quest to cover over the ugliness which I saw whenever I looked at myself in the mirror, at the real me naked and bare. I hated how I looked and despite time consuming episodes of applying the fake façade I was rarely satisfied with the results. Despite the exhausting ritual I continued to plaster on heavy foundation, eye shadow and lipstick as it seemed a much better option than what I looked like before. A hideous individual. I simply could not accept the reflection no matter how hard I tried and refused to believe that I had any real beauty, presence or definition. It was a distorted image which I always saw looking back at me and so it didn't matter how complimentary a friend or acquaintance might have been towards me, I could never bring myself to accept their words as truth. If anything it made me want to cover over more as I convinced myself that their words came as a result of really noticing something wrong as opposed to something good; and so I continued to plaster my face with layers upon layers of various different colours and shades which then began to affect my skin and caused acne. I felt trapped in the cycle of having to cover my face to the point where going without makeup was no longer an option even if I felt to have a day without it. The makeup often felt heavy and dragged me down so to speak, but still I carried on believing I had no other option. I refused to let the world see the real me for fear of further rejection, so I carried on with the suffocation – not only to my skin, but to my soul. In addition to my jaded perspective and the ever present need to cover up my face, I attempted to compensate even further in other ways and so the shift in pattern altered to that of other compulsive behaviours with my next obsession in the form of keeping fit and going to the gym. I would spend lengthy time there attending numerous classes back to back in an attempt to create a change in shape to my body. It allowed for many distractions, one of which saw keeping fit as a way to help make up for the failings in my face. I found great encouragement through exercise, but whilst it seemingly gave some short term gratification, it was never for any real length of time. As I got fitter I became even more self-aware, fixating on why it appeared that my body wasn't able to keep up as I looked at the shape of my stomach and the lack of muscle definition to my arms and legs. Once again I felt disappointed, but I was failing to see what was really happening as I complained to friends about how I was shaping up, much to their dismissal. Some jokingly returned the idea that I had developed body dysmorphic disorder and although it seemed utterly absurd, the diagnosis appeared to becoming true. I could not see anything but a failed attempt to be super lean and a better me and so I carried on almost seemingly determined to break myself into submission through exercise. I focused on clean eating and would train six days a week, sometimes twice a day in an attempt to gain results, but it all had minimal impact on my attitude towards myself. It was during this time that I also became interested in tattoos and piercings. I felt a longing to change something else and thought that perhaps I could do it in what I felt was a 'semi artistic way.' At first I pierced my belly button which made me feel more feminine, but once the feeling wore off I needed an alternative and so my next venture came in the form of a tattoo. The lily I had carved out on my lower back was to represent a new season and birth to a new life; a new me. The idea of change came after a bad breakup where I had initially left a relationship in an attempt to get a response from my then boyfriend Damien, who I felt lacked commitment, but it all went wrong. Following the breakup, he no longer wanted to be with me and went on to find someone else – someone who I saw as being much prettier and better than me, so I knew there was no going back. I hated myself for my impetuous behaviour and for what I thought was the biggest mistake of my life, as I was left to watch powerlessly in the background whilst his new relationship went from strength to strength. Nevertheless through the pain of yet another bad breakup I knew that I needed to move on and find a new lease of life, but instead of dealing with and facing some tough issues within me, I hid behind metal and ink, piercing and marking new beginnings on my skin. It hurt as the tattooist made his lines and shading to create the artwork, but as I sat through the pain of body art I found freedom in that very same pain which helped release the pain in my heart….albeit temporarily.

It didn't stop there. In an attempt to feel better about my body and more sexually alive and expressive, I then pierced my nipple and tongue. At this stage in my life I wanted to show people just how risqué and out there I could be, plus I wanted to prove myself as sexually adventurous rather than the ugly bore who couldn't keep a man and who lacked any real success in life. I wanted to see creativity on my helpless being and body art seemed the best way in which to achieve that. I also felt a sense of release as the painful experiences of the needle became a distraction. Friends questioned my motives for having so much work done in a short space of time asking if all was ok, but I would simply laugh off any of their concerns as being something I wanted to do for my own pleasure, however this was not true. My motives had always been for either attention or escape – neither being pleasurable nor the right choices, but still I carried on in a jaded attempt to find myself.

I also found it difficult to sustain a romantic relationship. It seemed as though the vast majority of my partners would often grow bored of me in quick succession, and this seemed to be the case no matter what I did. I convinced myself of needing to find a way to encourage their love and so I rationalised that I could do so by the giving of my pierced and tattooed body. This meant I would often indulge in sexual intimacy quite early on in the relationship in an attempt to gain approval, but the sexual act proved to be just that and not of love. I then became angry as nothing I did seemed to would work no matter how hard I tried. It did not matter how loving I had been towards my partner at the time or how well I put my makeup together; it did not matter how hard I worked at my body in the gym or how great I performed in bed as I created unhealthy soul ties, I still failed at gaining their love and was never quite good enough. As a result, I grew to a deepened level of bitterness and resentment after each failed relationship, feeling left with no option other than to continue on a road of self-destructive patterns of behaviour in a quest to find some kind of acceptance and love. In my frustration and dismay, I concluded that my way and understanding of how relationships were supposed to be had been wrong and the reason why I failed each and every time. It seemed that trying to be the nice girl, accommodating and low maintenance was proving to be of a disadvantage rather than a success and so I decided to try another way. I no longer wanted to be the one who lost out or the one to be used as I had felt, so I decided on another course of action. I felt it was time to go to war on these uncaring and unloving men, treating them in the same way they had always seen me. Disposable, I decided that I no longer wanted commitment, attachments or any kind of love - just sex. I convinced myself that I could "do it like a man" with no strings attached. I thought I would like the so-called power and release gained through my reckless actions; I wanted to be detached from my emotions and so far removed from any real relationship that I could not be hurt again. I wanted to use men in the same way I had previously felt used but the reality of it was that this power trip did not last long, in fact I ended up being the one to feel used and dirty as I would drive home from a night of so-called fun. In my further self-loathing, I anguished over what I thought were the remaining options in my very fragmented life. I had tried all methods of release but each time I felt further and further away from any victory or regaining a sense of control over what was left of it.

I was out of ideas and options, and just needed to distance myself from all of the hurt I had experienced and felt deeply in my heart. The trouble was that I had not yet recognised I was the main protagonist. Instead I blamed every person I believed was responsible for hurting me and determined that my insecurities came as a direct word or action from another; whilst certain situations assisted in opening flood gates filled with trauma, ultimately I had always been the one to step freely through them. In a desperate attempt to do something to help take the edge off the many fracture wounds of my emotions, again I toyed with the idea of exploring Christianity. I agreed to go to church with my friend Jason who had turned his life around and given it to Christ. He seemed to be growing confidently away from the street boy I had always seen him as in college, to a mature man of God and his encouragement allowed for some confidence within me, however his efforts did not work. Eventually they proved futile as I refused to accept the necessary changes and what I saw as hard work in order to become a born again believer. I believed that there were too many sacrifices in order to be right with God which I wasn't yet willing to make. I wasn't sure I even wanted to be anything with God anyway! I still wanted to do me - party, drink alcohol and have sex freely if I so pleased. So I walked away from any possibility of a new life in Christ and continued on living a miserable existence, remaining lost.

Despite the many unchanging and evident struggles, my life was not hard in comparison to that of others who may have suffered the real trauma of either losing loved ones or experiencing sexual and/or physical abuse. However I wasn't happy and the vast majority of everyday life events felt a continuing challenge without reprieve. It was then that I fell into a habit of abusing laxatives much to the further detriment of my mental and physical health. It all started simply with an idea for short term help. I managed to convince myself that taking laxatives was a good idea and the best way forward in order to help me lose weight quickly. I wanted to do something that was discreet and a less invasive way to get some control over my diet and in a way that no-one would even notice. I concluded that I could continue as I had always been, invisible to the naked eye, so it would be easy to get away with using laxatives. I also convinced myself that laxatives were the best alternative to other harsh methods of food extraction and would allow me complete control. It meant that I began to overindulge on different luxury foods or treats, often by binge eating. Unfortunately the food high was often followed by a very prominent low as I would feel disgusted with myself and then need to purge in an attempt to regain the control. I often felt a sense of freedom and a cleansing during the ritual of removal, as I was seemingly able to let go of all the things that were hurting me by clearing my body. The food was a reflection of all the debris in my life, but the so-called sense of winning would only last temporarily as the guilt over my actions brought on a feeling of bondage. I was stuck. The feeling of being unclean and self-loathing would return and so I would repeat the cycle in an attempt to 'chase the dragon' which allowed me to feel free. My actions went from a way to feel better, to habitual behaviour, to obsession. Soon enough I was unable to go a day without taking a concoction of laxatives. My trips to the supermarket had to include picking up a packet of my favourite daily fix and I would reach the shelves for laxatives as easily as selecting a carton of milk. It was as easy as that. I didn't care about what it was doing to me physically and I refused to think about it as I continued on in destroying my life.

Whilst taking the laxatives I was often left feeling unwell following a night of stomach cramps, night sweats and diarrhoea. It meant I would have to take time away from work as a result of the impending depression brought on by my actions. I could no longer control the sense of despair as it all began to forge a mighty big wall which I could neither climb over nor breakdown. It led to further disillusion about my life and a deeper sense of unhappiness which led to my doctor deeming it a necessary course of action to prescribe anti-depressants. I felt utter hopelessness, suffocated and confined with no way out. I ended up developing acute anxiety and would often cry uncontrollably prior to any trips away from my home. I felt I could not cope or face the world. I was of no benefit to anyone – family or friends, and with that in my already fragile mind, paranoia consumed me. I convinced myself that everyone I encountered would see through my craziness; as such I did not want to face that or anyone. It took over my whole way of thinking and I sank even further as I hid away from the entire world, still abusing my body with laxatives. The chemical dependency became a companion and friend, and one I simply would not give up. For many years I kept from loved ones what evidently became an eating disorder because I was ashamed of my secret. I knew that it would confirm that perhaps I was in fact mentally unstable which I was afraid of, but eventually I managed enough courage to confess the abuse of laxatives to those closest to me. Despite having to give up the laxatives and the subsequent vulnerability I felt being without them, I decided to face my demons and felt strong enough to begin counselling and after two years in continuous therapy I started to see some light. God however, was still not a factor in my life and I was still not prepared to look at my faith as an option for any form of release. I felt somewhat better, but did not attribute any of the positive emotions and better spirit to God's salvation and as a result there was little adjustment or any real improvement – I just learnt to cope better. Counselling helped facilitate better coping strategies without the need to abuse laxatives and whilst things were improving, there were some aspects of my life that evidently had not changed and I still felt as though something was missing. I could not make any connection between forgiving myself for past mistakes and letting go a little which would have allowed God to move in revelation over my life. So I carried on doing things the best way I thought how, but I was still left without peace.

A few years later my life had remained in much the same way with the acceptance of mediocrity being at the centre of my very existence, until I met 'Everything'. Before he came along there was a lack and a limit and a very evident need for something else to happen. It seemed that with his presence and ever growing influence came a real opportunity for a change in pace and a new direction. It was evident that my previous methodology had not worked so well and my life choices certainly had neither made me feel good about myself nor helped to identify any real sense of accomplishment. I pondered over the idea that perhaps in meeting 'Everything' I had a real chance to see a significant difference in my life with his help. I had been given a new hope and a brighter future through a man who was nothing but love and light. As I got to know him more and more and reflected on the possibilities, 'Everything' continued to win me over. Our first unofficial date saw him present me with three gifts; a bright pink covered bible, a personalised book called 'The Purpose Driven Life' and an RnB gospel CD. At first I did not know how to receive what he had given me as I had never known such attention, but as I sat across the table from him glancing down at the gifts laid out in front of me, a crumpled expression of questioning was soon replaced with a grateful smile as the feeling of butterflies floated around my stomach. I looked at him taking a deep breath and realised the gift that God had given me in the form of 'Everything' and for the first time in my life I felt that God had truly moved to present me with a blessing and I was thankful. From that point on, there were many more encounters and meetings with 'Everything'. He would often come to visit at my place of work to either just sit with me, bring lunch or to take me for walks. It was the ending of spring and the beginning of summer, and with the changing of seasons brought about opportunities to venture through local parks and just appreciate the world around us as we walked and talked, whilst getting to know each other more. With each lunch time visit came a greater understanding of 'Everything' including how he came to Christ. He explained about the various ministries he was involved with in his local church including worship, which he expressed a deep passion for. It seemed to form a solid root in his heart, but he also expressed a longing to go further in his ministry. 'Everything' wanted to be the very best he could be in Christ and explained that he, along with the church, were putting plans into motion to prepare him for a bigger ministry and more responsibility. I felt impressed however, equally inferior. Whilst I loved his expression of dedication and passion, I could only understand it from a selfish viewpoint. I questioned where I could possibly fit into his life if he was so dedicated in his love for God and devoted in church ministry. It was a very immature way of thinking but I didn't understand how he could possibly balance a "normal" life with both me and God in the picture and it rose insecurity within me. I was confused, but in my confusion I was not deterred enough to stay away. I believed that I had a good chance of coming out victorious in his priorities, by becoming first in his heart and was determined to succeed by becoming the best partner he could ever wish or pray for. However, there was another aspect which I had not given much thought to which caused other conflict in my mind. I knew there was a real chance to taste the possibility of a different life in Christ and I truly liked the idea of it. In my desire to become more knowledgeable, I began reading 'The Purpose Driven Life'. I wanted to grow in greater understanding of where 'Everything' was coming from in the hope of becoming more connected to his life. I wanted to understand his spiritual walk and view it as a positive – one that I didn't have to compete against. I also wanted some aspects of what he had in my own life, as I could see in him a confidence that was not engineered by money or popularity, but simply through peace and joy. At first reading the book was difficult. Not because it was complicated in its theory, but just because I struggled to digest the subject matter. I knew that there had to be something to it all and that as a Christian Catholic who believed in God there was meaning, but still I struggled. I had to dig deeper in my understanding, but I felt frustrated and disappointed because I just couldn't get it…really feel it. I questioned myself over why it felt so difficult when it should have been easily sinking in. I wanted to try and learn; I wanted to be there and try to understand where 'Everything' was coming from, but still I struggled greatly. However I pressed on determined to experience the same warmth behind his smile which I knew had to have come from somewhere, so I carefully planned out my next move and pondered the idea of visiting his church. Sometime earlier, 'Everything' had invited me to attend but I quickly made up an excuse as to why I couldn't, claiming other commitments which mostly formed part of my weekly gym routine. However, I felt a pull and an urge to go and so I decided to surprise him one Sunday.

The day I went was nerve racking. It was such a big deal for me to take any kind of positive step towards God and I can remember feeling close to light headed. My heart was racing as I pulled up outside the church. It was like going to take a final exam that I was unsure of passing and I felt overwhelmed. It was such a big building and instantly I felt very self-conscious as I walked into the main foyer. It almost felt as if people would automatically recognise me as a "non-believer" and judge me on my motives for being there without knowing anything about me. The more I juggled around endless thoughts centred on judgement, the more doubtful I felt and I toyed with the idea of leaving. However, just the thought of seeing a look of pleasant surprise from 'Everything' was enough to bring me back to focus. So I carried on into the main auditorium and as I entered the sheer scale of size and the amount of people that were part of the congregation was overwhelming. I wanted to sit down quickly hopefully going unnoticed as a newbie, but everyone was standing and singing in worship to God, so sitting was not an option. Despite the discomfort, I remained standing whilst I scanned the stage area looking for 'Everything' but I could not see him where I expected to, singing on the stage with the worship team.

I continued looking around for him, scanning the entire auditorium and then back to the stage viewing the worship team again to see if I had overlooked him, but he was nowhere to be seen. It quickly became obvious he was not there and as the realisation hit me, my heart sank. I had made a special trip with the primary intention of seeing him but it had been in vain and in my frustration, I neglected to acknowledge that the true purpose of my attendance should have been solely to meet with God, not anyone else. As I sat down I felt myself disconnecting from the service as I realised how distracted I had become by the absence of 'Everything'. In an attempt to shake it off I tried to bring my thoughts back to thinking about God as I began to concentrate on listening to the pastor with intention. As the service continued however, I found my mind wondering from thinking about 'Everything', back to the sermon, to then looking around the congregation in judgement as soon as I heard a powerful "Amen!" or "Hallelujah!". It was difficult to focus on the word of God and I felt frustrated over my inability to follow or pay attention to it. I felt as though I were back at school during a class I had little to no interest in, squirming around as if I had ants in my pants. I felt like a child with no discipline or maturity and I did not like it.

I wanted to go home. It felt pointless being somewhere I didn't fit in. As I discreetly gathered my belongings intent on leaving, I felt the smallest urge of something….a pull even. I attempted to ignore it as I crept out of the service but I could feel an increasing presence of a whisper in my heart which steadily grew the closer I got to the exit door. Suddenly, I was stopped in my tracks by a member of the ministry team who wanted to have a chat with me to welcome my visit to the church. My instinct was to lie and say that I had to rush off, but the ever present still whispering voice wouldn't allow me to, and so I accepted the invitation to stay and talk for a little while longer. The conversation seemed to ignite a feeling deep within that left me with a sense of indescribable peace. It was as if a built up pressure had instantly been lifted and made space for something else. I wasn't sure what that something actually was, but I could feel a sense of power in what I imagined was that silent whisper of encouragement within my heart. There was a sense of prosperity on the horizon and my soul felt as if it were coming alive. I left the church feeling lighter. It was only a small difference, but a definite one. Somehow in that very moment it did not matter that 'Everything' had not been there. I had discovered something which made me feel good about me, even if just for that moment. I began deliberating with myself about the possibility of exploring the church further. Was it really something too difficult to be around or could I challenge myself by stepping into a new arena? After all, if feeling good – refreshed and anew in my spirit could be so effortless, what could be so hard about giving it a try? Still I wasn't sure, but I thought about my life and what I achieved by my own efforts, which reflected little progression. I thought about how lonely I had been in the past and how much I didn't want to go back to the previous hurts and mistakes. My life had never been all singing and dancing down the yellow brick road – it had been tough emotionally, but now there was more to come. Not only did I have 'Everything' and the beginning of a new love relationship, but there was another element….the possibility of God entering in to my very existence. I knew that I didn't have all the tools, I knew that I didn't fully understand and that I would struggle with learning a new way of life, but I wanted to give it a try.

I made a decision there and then to return to church the following week, knowing I would have 'Everything' and that going deeper was never more appealing.

CHAPTER 5

Going Deeper

It didn't take very long for things to progress at a rapid pace in our newly appointed relationship, propelling myself and 'Everything' into an unbreakable bond. We did all that we could together, spending every available moment with each other and we quickly became inseparable. With each waking moment we grew closer and closer, becoming more and more involved in each other's lives. As the weeks went by turning into months it quickly grew to a point where I started to limit seeing friends. I became less engaged in spending time with them and hanging out because my priorities had changed. It wasn't a conscious decision as such, but I was very much in awe of 'Everything' and totally in love with my new relationship, so much so that nothing else seemed to matter. I rationalised missing dates with friends and letting them down as "ok." I was in a new relationship and of course they would understand, but the complaints from friends and family over my lack of presence became more frequent. I embarrassingly made up excuses time and time again, apologising for my absence but also dismissing their ideas as folly. However there was also a small part of me that knew I was making a point blank and deliberate choice between them and 'Everything'. This, I could never admit out loud. Unfortunately these choices cost me some friendships, but again I was too focused on my new relationship with 'Everything' to care. Any time spent with him was at the forefront of my thoughts and actions and took priority over anything else. All I wanted to do was spend every waking moment that I could with him and I wasn't willing to allow anything to interfere. I prioritised 'Everything' much to the detriment of friendships and a breakdown in communication with loved ones.

In the beginning of my relationship with 'Everything' I still had my own home which I shared with a friend but that did not alter any of the time I would spend with my new found love. 'Everything' would regularly come over and spend time with me, spending days at a time where we would just hang out, cook, clean and do all the regular things I guess you would say a couple do together. 'Everything' was enthusiastic about wanting to make my home and life better and there would be times I would come home to flowers in my room or I would drive home and he would be there in the garden weeding up plants and clearing rubbish

which always impressed me (although I never let him know that).
It was just so nice to have someone in my life that didn't have to be
told what to do or how to do it, but someone who just knew what
I needed – that was 'Everything'. I think the type of relationship
we entered in to was new to both myself and 'Everything' but
more so him. It was the first time in experiencing a real grown
up, committed relationship, and so there was an even deeper
desire within him to see it flourish and do well. It seemed as if
our relationship was at the forefront of his efforts. This was very
evident in his actions. Until the point of meeting me, I don't think
he had been with a woman before who was older, more mature in
approach to life and fiercely independent, so this too, I believed,
was a driving force behind his will to make me happy and succeed
in his efforts. I also firmly believed that 'Everything' wanted to see
my own personal relationship with Christ grow not only because
he knew how important it was for me, but also for us to be in a
committed relationship together led only by God. His very detailed
efforts brought forth something which I had not anticipated…I was
falling deeply for him and I couldn't ignore the ignited passion I
felt towards him. It was love. I was falling in love and it wasn't long
before I felt as if there was no place I would rather be. Not only did
I want to be his girlfriend – I wanted more and so I quickly made
up my mind that not only did I see a future for us but I saw him as
my life partner and soul mate.

I had never before in my life experienced a man so loving
towards me; one who was enthusiastic about me, accepting me just

the way I was. I did not have to do much to have his attention and focus because he seemed not to care about the little indiscretions, how I looked or how I dressed…he was fully accepting of me just as I was. His acceptance of me gave me great sense of confidence and ownership over the relationship. I felt secure and I felt sure of his feelings towards me. I felt sure of who he was, I felt sure of who I was and in-turn I felt sure of where we were and who we were to each other.

I have to give thanks to God, because I knew even in the very early stages of my spiritual journey and immaturity that 'Everything' was a gift from, and sent by God. All that he would do was imparted by the Holy Spirit. 'Everything' acted as a clear demonstration of God's love, and such blessings went hand in hand with all the other recent experiences and encounters; simply put, in Jesus Christ. 'Everything' was encompassing of it all, and it made me feel alive and refreshed. It was very exciting. I carried on going to church with him on a more regular basis wanting to experience the inner peace and joy as I felt increasingly confident to do so, but then there would be issues surrounding that. You see, I was going "deeper"….learning more about God, learning more about Christ and mostly, learning more what it meant to be in a relationship with God through Jesus Christ. But over all of that and at the forefront, I was going deeper with 'Everything'. However, my new relationship was at the centre and that was before anything else - not the way it should have been.

I can remember my lack of commitment to going to church; I would arrive late, thinking that was ok because after all, in my mind, I was finally being proactive in church life, growing more confidently and getting into a routine with good habits. This was all wrong. I mostly loved the idea of going to church with him as a couple and that's where the motivation came from, but there was something that was missing and not quite right. I still wasn't willing to give up certain aspects of my day to day life and routine especially on a Sunday. Firstly, I was adamant that I would only go to church on a Sunday evening. My reasoning for that initially was that I "preferred" to go to church in the evening as opposed to the morning service. I would state the point that the morning services were too overwhelming, whereas the evening sessions were more quiet and intimate. I could tell in the beginning that 'Everything' was a bit confused and somewhat disappointed that I wouldn't go to the morning services, but in his endeavour to help keep me focused and supported, he would attend with me in the evenings. I could tell that he wanted me to grow in confidence, so he would often double up on his attendance at church. I greatly respected him for it but at the same time, I couldn't understand his persistence. In truth, I think I grew to understand but rejected his intentions for my growth, so there would be times where I would cancel at the last minute proclaiming that I was too tired to attend. 'Everything' would never verbalise it, but I could always see the disappointment in his face. I think that was one of the things I found hardest – not that I was disappointing God, but that I was disappointing 'Everything'.

The reason for my lack of attendance to the morning services was because I loved going to the gym on a Sunday to do my Step Aerobics and Legs, Bums and Tums classes. So I thought a fair compromise would be to do my own thing in the morning, and deal with God's business in the evening – albeit half-heartedly. Still, I rationalised that I was doing what was fair for both God and I; I felt good about it, but what a fool I was. There was no room for God to enter into my heart, because my heart was not yet with Him. The thing is, as time went on, I felt as if I was going deeper, but I was only going deeper with 'Everything' whilst my relationship with God and going to church was flagging behind. I wasn't making the same level of effort with church and seeking God as I was with 'Everything' because my focus, primarily, was on my earthly relationship and not my spiritual one. But as a Christian and a Born Again believer, I knew that that was not it. It was always supposed to be Jesus at the centre, and God before anything. But I wasn't acting in accordance with that core belief and Christian value and it quickly became a problem in the relationship.

There was much conflict between myself and 'Everything'. We had so many different viewpoints about things that quickly became obvious during various discussions and in each of our own actions. Whilst I was going to church and making an obvious start on my spiritual journey with a willingness to develop this by growing in my relationship with God through Jesus, I still wasn't willing to give up my fleshly habits whereas 'Everything' had. I would still pursue things that I shouldn't; sleeping over at each other's homes, pre-marital sex and pursuing 'Everything' in ways that went against God's commands. At times I felt sorry for 'Everything' as he tried hard to encourage better practises and to keep to God's ways by being disciplined in our spiritual walks. But as I fought against it in the name of love for him, it became increasingly difficult for 'Everything' as his love for me became a greater distraction and a spiritual stumbling block. I was guilty of making things more difficult for him as I could feel myself falling in love with him on a deeper level, so I wanted more of him.

Often, 'Everything' would make the decision to not stay over and go home or say he didn't want to sleep with me, leaving me feeling rejected. These disagreements increased as time went on and the sense of abandonment and rejection became entrenched. It was really tough for both of us, but I never considered how he might be feeling or if he was in fact struggling himself – all I cared about and all I could see was simple; I cared about and loved him and he seemed to love and care about me, so why couldn't we be together in every way? It seemed simple. The problem was that it was a constant battle between wanting the sexual intimacy, to wanting to do what was right - the battle between flesh and spirit. It caused us to lose our way with each other and more importantly with God. I saw no problem with us being together in such a way because I saw things as moving forward and I saw a definite long term future with 'Everything'. I was excited about what I interpreted as a developing Christian relationship, but the problem was that the type of relationship that 'Everything' and I were developing, although filled with love in the beginning, it was not God's way.

Within the first year of our relationship, we decided to move in together. At the beginning my whole philosophy behind the theory of moving in together was based on our conversations regarding our vision for the future. 'Everything' and I had discussed long term goals, so it seemed to make perfect sense to progress that by moving in and setting up a home to further cement our commitment. In my thinking, the focus was purely upon building a future with him and I didn't even begin to consider nor acknowledge the spiritual understanding of what moving in together prior to being married actually meant. All I could think about was what I wanted and what I thought was right - marriage and children, and what it took to get there. I figured that if we moved in together, "I" could save up and then we could have a wedding and get married ....I didn't even give a second thought to what 'Everything' thought about it deep down inside, and or if he even wanted to get married. I didn't consider what this all may have been doing to him spiritually, because my understanding came from a completely different direction. His decision to move in with me was not in alignment with the core values and beliefs of the church and as a result affected his position in leadership, as our living together did not set a good example. There were things that

had to be sacrificed in his position at church following us moving
in together; 'Everything' had to make the difficult choice to stand
down from being part of the Worship and Sunday School teaching
Teams, which I now understand troubled him deeply. Although
it was difficult, 'Everything' made the choice himself because he
wanted to do what he felt was responsible and right. At the time, I
was ignorant to it all. If anything I just rationalised it and tried to
make my peace with God about it all through prayer but this was
not enough....as I later learned the hard way. You see, to give up
something FOR God brings great reward, but to give up on God's
way in order to pursue your own can do nothing but bring great
peril and sorrow. I came to understand that no matter what you
may try to do by your own strength and apart from God, will only
seek to fail. In John 15:5 (NIV) says: - "I am the vine; you are the
branches. If you remain in me and I in you, you will bear much
fruit; apart from me you can do nothing."

It was evident that 'Everything' and I were beginning
on a road apart from His guidance, trying to work out our own
interpretation of His will and His way as opposed to following
His guidance, but it was never with the intention not to love God.
I knew confidently that I was beginning to fall in love with The
Father and despite some of my very misguided ways and warped
perception, there was progress. With each waking moment I grew
closer, reaching further and digging deeper. I knew that I had a
friend in Jesus and that I could take anything to Him in prayer.

Granted, I did not fully understand who I should be to Him or what He was to me, but I was learning; and in my learning, I began to receive Him. I began to feel His healing. I was rising up towards Him on what felt like the strength of eagle's wings. There was an outpouring of the Holy Spirit and with that, my barriers and restrictions were being removed and being replaced with a growing desire to go deeper.

CHAPTER 6

A Promise to Love

About a year and a half into my relationship with 'Everything', a few things started to happen. My love for 'Everything' felt completely established – at its peak, whilst my love for God was merely creeping forward at a much slower pace instead of developing and growing in depth as it should have been. Despite the clear contradiction in priorities between my love for God and for the man that was 'Everything', I believed in my heart that the love I felt for both my Father and my boyfriend were pure and true. I wanted my commitment to be equally established and demonstrated in my daily life, but there remained an obvious imbalance. The very evident problem was that I knew in my heart I had placed 'Everything' before God because I believed that my earthly love deserved more effort. 'Everything' was tangible and it was him who helped me on the road to becoming a better person, so in light of the fact I saw it as more acceptable to love in the flesh than in that of the spirit. It was what had felt right to me from the beginning but I desperately wanted to change as I began to grow in greater conviction over the conflict in my priorities. The more I grew to understand God's ways through His word, developing in intimacy with the Father and building on my relationship with Him, the more powerful a desire began to build within me towards God. I wanted Him to be first in all aspects of my life; the first of my thoughts as I woke up, my confidence, my strength and my love. I wanted God to have all of me and not just what was left over once I had taken care of the needs of 'Everything'. I knew that my priorities were questionable but still I fought daily with taking any real responsibility for a lack of commitment towards God. I would try to either completely ignore or justify my lack of commitment to The Father, but with that came a greater conviction in my spirit. My deeds and actions felt as if they were continually failing God each and every day I would make the choice to place 'Everything' before Him. In truth, I knew that God had left it all in my hands – to make my own choices in life and to take the direction which I thought was right. He allowed me to decide where I would stand and gave me the choice to walk the path I had decided as best. As I reflected over how gracious and merciful God had always been towards me despite my failings, it made me speechless in the realisation that He continued to bless me irrespective of where I stood. I would gasp at His awesomeness in the realisation that He loved me without limit even though I had placed so many limits on Him. I couldn't help but pause and reassess my heart towards The Father, as I acknowledged the fact that His capacity was endless. Just the thought of His resilience and patience with me took my breath away and as I took a moment to pause in contemplation, it reduced me to tears. The tears that opened the floodgates of a deeper emotion were not tears of sadness, but tears in the realisation of His unfailing love. I was truly blessed and as I sat in deeper reflection of both my relationship with God and with 'Everything', I knew that it was by no accident that they had both touched my life in such a significant way; as I continued on in a time of reflection, I reminisced over the very first moments that I finally sat up and took notice of both God and 'Everything' with a clear and very loving understanding of the role they played in my heart, which was to change my life forever and create in me a promise.

Part one – A Promise to 'Everything'

It was a cold, frosty and uneventful winter's morning. The weather forecast had predicted a heavy downpour of snow, but as I looked out of the window in anticipation and up into the grey sky, it all seemed calm and motionless. Without an obvious sign of a single snowflake, I decided to dismiss the impending storm as folly and continued on with my Saturday plans for training. Having made arrangements to meet with 'Everything' some time later, I headed off to the gym. Nonetheless, the weather took a turn for the worse and as predicted the snow began crashing down unexpectedly at an alarming rate, creating havoc on London's streets. Through all the traffic and chaos I somehow managed to get back to a meeting point with 'Everything' as we then attempted to make the drive back home however the weather became increasingly treacherous as the snow raged in its anger falling faster and heavier. The downpour of snowflakes fell to the ground thick and fast, settling at an alarming rate which took all drivers caught in it by surprise. There was no escaping as the snow covered local streets with thick layers of a cold, white blanket. There was no time allowed for the local council to dispatch trucks to grit the road aiding its safety as the snow continued to batter the surrounding areas, making it impossible to fight back and drive through it all. As a result, the streets began steadily backing up for miles with gridlocked traffic, as cars either remained stagnant or hemmed in by the growing height of snow. I watched on as wheels slipped on the icy slush and drivers desperately attempted to navigate their vehicles to safety through the treacherous conditions.

It seemed impossible for anyone to get very far.

As I sat in my car with 'Everything' trying patiently to wait out the storm, there was little to no progress as we edged forward at a snail's pace through the growing nightmare of gridlocked traffic. Whilst I tried to engage him in idle chit chat I could see that 'Everything' was distracted replying hesitantly in his responses. As I continued on in my angst, complaining about the snow and traffic, he gazed out of the window and then back in my direction with a growing look of concern on his face. He began to express that he was worried over the growing number of people he predicted would need help. Cars were swerving and there was little room to manoeuvre forcing cars into close and dangerous contact with each other. That was the thing about 'Everything'; he was attentive to the needs of others and would not just sit by and watch if he could support someone. He always wanted to help those who couldn't help themselves – to be a hero for the weak and for those who were placed in difficult situations that required rescue and so it seemed as though in that very moment of a storm, came an opportunity which would allow 'Everything' to become just that: a hero. As he continued on expressing his heartfelt concerns for all the drivers caught in the snow, stuck and unable to move in their vehicles, suddenly he decided that he wanted to help; without giving it a second thought 'Everything' keenly got out of my car, rushed off and disappeared in amongst the traffic before I could say very much to convince him otherwise.

I sat there thinking he was crazy as I replayed the words in my mind of his desire to help out by pushing vehicles. Despite his good intentions, I could not understand why he would want to suffer the cold and wet weather especially as his clothes weren't particularly appropriate for the chilling winter we were faced with. I could only put it down to temporary madness! He had no gloves on, nor did he have on appropriate footwear and, as he ran off into the pursuing downpour, I was completely perplexed and struggled to understand his persistence - but then I remembered something he had told me. Previously and sometime during the early part of our relationship, 'Everything' had explained that apart from his day to day ministry as a Christian, he believed that God had given him great strength in order that he could help people and as I reflected further on our conversations it all made sense. He wanted to be the one to help the helpless because it was what he understood to be part of his purpose in life and one of the many things God had intended for him. The reminder made me smile, and as I relaxed back into my chair meditating on the idea of such a powerful notion, a feeling of acceptance came over me as I waited out the traffic and for his return.

I sat waiting somewhat impatiently for 'Everything' to make his way back to me, but as the time racked up and he was nowhere to be seen, I pondered over what may have happened to him. He had been gone for some time without making contact, and with each passing minute came a greater concern within me for his well-being. The traffic began moving, edging forward to the pace of a crawl and as it continued creeping along eventually I could see 'Everything' in the distance doing exactly what he had said – pushing cars and buses through the snow with the assistance of others who I can only assume were encouraged by his actions. Relieved to see that he was alright and impressed by his endeavours, I called out his name loudly. He turned to acknowledge me and with authority and an obvious presence amidst his peers, he instructed me to drive further in the direction of home which I readily followed. As I continued crawling along in my faithful car Betty, eventually the traffic eased and the road cleared enough that I could get to a safe place to pull up and park. Quickly, I switched off my engine and reached impatiently for my mobile phone to make a call to 'Everything' but I could not get through to him and with each unsuccessful attempt to call came a growing sense of unrest. I thought the worst had happened – that he had been hurt and with that came the decision that I needed to find him. Fully armed with gloves, a coat and snow boots, I decided to get out of my car and began trudging through the elements in search of my 'Everything'. As I fought against the elements trying to focus enough to look through the sleet with squinted eyes, there he was in the distance walking towards me. It was clear that he was cold, tired and somewhat out of breath, but with each word out and deep exhalation there was an air of excitement and a sense of proud accomplishment in his voice as he recalled pushing the bigger vehicles to safety. He felt a sense of duty in continuing on with helping despite the fact that his trainers were completely soaked through and that his hands were cold to frozen, as it was visible to me that the blood had drained away to leave a paler complexion. Nevertheless, none of that mattered to him. He was not yet ready to throw in the towel whist all I wanted to do was get home and for us to wrap up together cosily with a hot drink and a blanket. I wasn't motivated to think about the needs of others in that moment, rather the fact that I was ruining my brand new snow boots which were beginning to fall victim to the weather. As we walked and he talked, I listened to him recount his snow stories whilst trying to navigate the developing frosty slush on the footpath. There were still a number of cars struggling to drive up the steady incline in the direction to which we were walking which we both noticed, but before I could say another word he was off making his way towards the first car stuck in the line-up. As he made his way to the rear of the vehicle, he looked like a Marvel superhero – big and strong as he began pushing against it with all the strength he had left in him. As 'Everything' battled against the weight of the metal and the ice on the ground, his efforts seemed futile; his feet slipped back whilst he fought against losing his grip, but still he carried on. He would simply not give in. That was 'Everything'. He was not a quitter and did not go back on his word. If he made a decision to do something and see it through, he would….and so he did that day. I watched on as he pushed on, and I could see the painful expression of exhaustion on his face, but still he would not quit. With cheeks puffed out and eyes closed, he extended the weight of his arms against the vehicle and I could begin to see progress. Slowly, the car began to move up the incline and as I watched him give all that he had to help a stranger, I felt motivated by his actions. Suddenly, I felt a very evident pull to do the same and in that very moment I too wanted to help. I also wanted to support him in helping others and be that beacon of light. I no longer cared about my new boots or wanting to get home or do anything else that involved putting me first, I just wanted to support my 'Everything'. Before I could give it another thought I was right there beside him and as he pushed I pushed, and before we knew it the struggling vehicle was up and over the hump of the snowy incline. As the driver thanked us we jokingly high fived each other, acknowledging our team effort but as we turned back to continue on in the direction of home, we paused for thought over the line-up of other cars still stuck on the incline. As we both looked at each other, we knew instinctively what we needed to do and so we continued on pushing each vehicle up the incline one by one. I can remember looking down at my boots which were completely saturated by icy slush feeling slightly perplexed, but then looking back at 'Everything' and not even questioning the trade-off. It felt good to be some sort of help in partnership with my own personal hero who was now in-turn a superhero to a large number of strangers who did not know who he was nor would they ever know, but it didn't matter because I knew who he was. I looked back down at my wet boots and shrugged as I looked back up in acknowledgement that I had something far better.

We continued on in the cold for some time pushing cars continuously one by one, and with each car cleared to safety there was a growing sense of purpose. It felt as if we were out there trying to make a difference; giving back to, and supporting a community so to speak. It wasn't even a conscience effort, it wasn't even one where we were trying to gain some kind of reward – we just wanted to help people. I also knew that when I looked at

'Everything' and saw a look of sheer determination on his face to help people, it made me even more determined to be by his side. I saw a real strength in him; not just a physical strength but strength in character and a real strength in his spirit which had to have come from God. It made me look at him with a fresh pair of eyes and appreciate 'Everything' in a way I had not yet realised. That day he also taught me something about selfless love and as silly or as clichéd as it might sound, it felt so good to just care for and love people simply by helping to push their cars up a hill. It was even more incredible seeing the look of surprise and then a look of humbled gratitude on the drivers' faces. You could see that they were shocked beyond comprehension by our actions. Each of the faces carried a look of amazement, as if each person had never received kindness or help in such a way before, and perhaps they never had. For me I felt a move of God for each person we encountered and every car that we pushed. I felt that God had used us to allow people to experience a light sprinkling and delicate touch of the Holy Spirit, letting people know that there was still good people in the world and more importantly that God is alive and very much present in all our lives.

During our time out in the elements, 'Everything' and I had reached a stage of feeling cold to frozen. My boots and his trainers were completely soaked through and our hands were stiff from touching the ice cold metal, but still we carried on. It was as if we could not move from that spot. We physically could not stop ourselves from pushing those cars to safety. We had easily been out in the snow for an hour or more, and if we had decided to stop there and then we could've happily moved on with our heads held high, satisfied in knowing that we had done our very best, but we just couldn't go. With each car that we pushed, there was another and then another which needed help. The cars just kept on coming and so we kept on pushing despite our tiredness. Just then, and quite literally out of nowhere, we were joined by a small Asian man who added his contribution to our cause by helping to push the cars. He politely introduced himself and said that he was a resident on the road and went on to explain that he had seen us pushing the cars out of his window and decided to help. He seemed keen and eager to join us and without a second thought he was right there next to us with a big smile on his face adding his contribution. Before long there was another resident of the street who came out to help us and then a lady appeared with a tray of hot chocolate saying she too had seen us and so decided to make the drinks to help keep us warm. Not long after that there were even more residents pouring out of their homes and into the snow to help us push cars and clear the snow enough so that drivers could get through easier. Suddenly there was a movement and a sea of people; husbands, wives, children and friends in abundance, all in a selfless act of helping others. It was the greatest show of community spirit and selfless love I had ever witnessed. God was working through His people in such a powerful way and it all started with just one man...'Everything'.

We were out in the snow until it began to get dark,
remaining until practically every car possible had been pushed
to safety and the road was clear for cars to continue on without
assistance. Exhausted, we made our way home and although
we were fuelled by the day, we remained silent in what felt like
an air of disbelief. As we tried to get warm, it was obvious that
we remained somewhat shocked and subdued by what had just
happened. Neither of us could believe what we had just witnessed
and what we had encouraged....a whole neighbourhood to action.
As 'Everything' and I sat back over a meal recalling the day's
events, neither of us felt boastful or talked with an air of pride – we
were both just amazed at what God had done. It was beautiful to
witness small children with their shovels and the parents joining
in unison to reach a common goal in helping those in need. It was
not something you witnessed every day and 'Everything' and I
were lucky enough with being blessed to be a wonderful great part
of it. It felt as if God had chosen us specifically to lead, motivate,
encourage and inspire, and in that very moment I felt a strong sense
of God's purpose for us together as a couple. I felt as if we had been
placed together to help change the hearts of those we encountered
collectively and it made me very excited. Not only that, but it made
me fall deeper in love with 'Everything'. I was reminded of a verse
in the Book of Proverbs 27:17 which says "As iron sharpens iron,
so one person sharpens another" and in that very moment I knew
instinctively that our purpose was clear. 'Everything' and I were to

be the iron to and for each other, to grow stronger through our life experiences together with God's help.

It was the first time I acknowledged a real acceptance within myself of what I truly felt towards him. It was my first real affirmation of love for 'Everything' and the day I set my feelings for him upon a rock. I never openly admitted anything to the effect, but that day changed something inside me. When I saw a clear look in his eyes of selflessness and to an extent, sacrifice, was the day I pledged to love him no matter the season. I had known before that I really, really liked him, but until that particular day I never knew that I truly loved him. He was my hero. He was my strength. He was one that could move mountains and change the hearts of people and that came because he was a man of faithful diligence and obedience to God. It was not simply because he was a regular man with a bit of strength behind him, but because he was moved to action and influence by the Holy Spirit. For me, that was the greater attraction. It was complete adoration, respect and a desire which developed right in that very moment towards 'Everything'. To see a man doing all that he could to help people without expecting anything back to the point it moved me to action along with a number of others, created a calling....and I had to answer it with my promise to love him.

Part Two - A Promise to God

It was a dull and boring Sunday. I didn't know what I wanted to do with the day, but I wasn't motivated to do very much. Often on a day where I felt lethargic and with no agenda, I would go to bingo to alleviate my boredom and take my mind elsewhere. I knew that gambling was not the done thing as a Christian and certainly not good for me financially or otherwise, but I wanted the distraction and so I began getting myself dressed and ready to go. As I dragged on my jeans and pulled on a jumper I kept hearing a voice; not an audible voice as such, but more of a whisper and a sense of my conscience telling me not to go. A part of me was in agreement – that I should have remained at home but there was that other rebellious part of me still wanting to go so I tried to shut the voice out by ignoring it, filling my head with the thoughts of a lucky win instead of following the voice of sensible reasoning. I finished getting ready, jumped in my car and headed off in the direction of Cricklewood, North West London. I reached for the CD player with confidence but as I switched it on my confidence changed to conviction as I remembered that I had left a CD recording of a service from church that had been playing earlier. As I listened to the sermon, it was all about being intentional and doing things for God and His people with meaning. I listened on as it talked about growing in a deeper commitment to God through our actions and

100

with each word I reflected on the irony of the situation I faced at that very moment. I felt guilty that I was going to gamble - going to do something that was not good for me, but I still wanted to do what I wanted to do. I began to feel ashamed as I heard Pastor Geoff repeat over the theme of living a life of intention. I wanted to eject the CD, chuck it away and play something else…anything else, but I couldn't. I wanted to drown out the voice of the messenger but it was as if I were physically unable to do so. It was as if my hands were locked to the steering wheel and I could not do anything to stop it. I was forced to hear it.

As I continued driving along a road to nowhere, I became more frustrated in my spirit. I continued on with a growing sense of guilt to the point that it shrouded me in shame. The closer I got to my destination, the more increasingly uncomfortable I became. It was weird, as if there was a spiritual pull between my fleshly desire to go and my spiritual desire to resist…fight against it; the more I had a stirring in my heart and mind between the right and wrong choice, the more conflicted I felt. In the background the CD was still playing with the voice of Pastor Geoff coming through very clearly, reinforcing the message of intention and commitment. He went on to speak about a stage in every Christian's spiritual life where the voice of God and His calling on our lives can no longer be ignored and we have to respond. It felt as if the message had been written just for me. It was so apt for where I was; not only as a believer but in that very moment driving my car to bingo and it was no coincidence. I knew that I should have turned back in the direction of home but the rebellious nature of my flesh made me carry on. That was the thing about me; sometimes I would hear something stirring in my mind or feel some conviction in my heart which was ultimately guiding me away from sin and to another place that was for my greater good, but I would purposely ignore it. I would actively turn onto the wrong path knowing it would hurt me, but would still do it almost as if I deliberately wanted to trip myself up. It made no sense to hurt myself and it certainly made no sense to try and ignore the Holy Spirit, but there I was. I carried on driving pressing on in the wrong direction but with each mile added to my journey, the more aggressive I felt in my spirit and in my mind. I was angry, annoyed and irritated. I was irritated by the words coming through the CD player about commitment, intention and purpose…the words kept stirring around, circling over and over again as Pastor Geoff spoke with passion and his voice becoming louder. I couldn't drown it out no matter how hard I tried and in not being able to block out each word spoken with authority, I felt more frustrated towards the situation I faced in the growing guilt. However there was a sudden shift and it felt as if I could begin to hear and feel God's words resonating within me. As I drove on I felt almost as if I were in a comatose state, catatonic and dazed. I felt hypnotised by the reoccurring words of what began to sound like truth. I began to accept that perhaps the journey I had decided to make was not going to produce good fruit. Perhaps the intended enticement of a financial windfall through gambling which I had readily accepted not an hour or so before, was now like the taste of vinegar instead of a fine wine. I began opposing it. Not only had the opposition stirred up a sense of rejection, I still retained some sort of feeling of frustration and in my frustration I lost focus and almost crashed my car into another driver's vehicle. The near miss led to a heated exchange with the other driver including windows wound down, gesturing and the use of profanity as we both cursed at each other. After driving off and then parking up, I wound up my window, sat back in my seat and exhaled in reflection as the sheer measure of the argument consumed me with further guilt. I questioned myself over my thoughts and actions as I acknowledged my act of aggression was inappropriate and not in alignment with either God's word or who I trying to be at that point in my life. Granted, I wasn't perfect but I wanted to be a better person and an example of what it meant to be a Christian and not some wild woman without any filter or morals. I felt awful and my mood descended further. I questioned if I still wanted to go into bingo and if I could even still go in. As I began walking to towards the main entrance I felt grimy, greasy and dirty – filthy even. I felt as if I had been saturated in some kind of crude oil which continued to weigh me down with every step I took. My body felt heavier as if it were weighing into the ground. It felt as if I were dragging a heavy ball and chain which slowed me down more and more, but just as I got to the entrance door tired and worn out ready to cross the threshold, something stopped me completely in my tracks. It felt as if someone had physically placed their hand out across my chest, protecting me. I looked towards the bright lights and slot machines as they rang out in unison, and I could hear the enticing voice of the bingo caller but I could not move to take another step. Something inside me said "no" and in that instance I turned back around to the direction of my car and then home. With each step I took away from the bingo hall, I felt lighter and the imaginary ball and chain lifted being replaced with a feeling of wanting to run free and so I got back in my car and I drove in the direction of home.

As I drove home I was reminded of a distinct pain I had been experiencing for the best part of the day. An ongoing injury to my shoulder and neck had flared up causing discomfort with the pain steadily creeping down my arm. Not only that, but I still felt as though I needed something but wasn't sure what it was. I drove home feeling confused and somewhat perplexed, but there was also a real sense of relief within me in making the decision to turn away from the enticement of the Las Vegas style lights and noises of the bingo hall. I felt a sense of victory over the flesh but there was something still niggling at me that I desperately needed freeing from. As I drove back, I thought about going to church as an option for a release but I wasn't sure if I should - especially after where I had just come from but by the time I got home there was a real growing sense of need inside of me. The pain was no longer just in my shoulder but also in my mind; I felt a battle, being torn between where I had just been and where I should go. I tried to make a decision to go to church, but my thoughts were clouded as something kept pulling me back convincing me not to. I could hear a voice inside my head coming up with excuses as to why I should just stay home. I thought about calling 'Everything' as a distraction but I knew in that moment that I could not tell him what was going on or where I had just been, as I knew he did not approve of me going to bingo in the first place. He never tried to stop me from going, but he knew that it was not good for me spiritually, so whenever I would go I would avoid telling him or would ignore his calls if he happened to contact me whilst I was there. I decided not to call him but instead just stood there to try and find a moment of clarity. I could hear a voice telling me to stay home and just relax, convincing me I was tired and so I began talking myself out of going to church, but then there was another more prominent voice telling me to go; telling me that I needed to be encouraged and that there was something for me at church...a gift. I felt a sudden burst of excitement which stirred up in my spirit, but there was a continued distraction as I went back and forth between deciding to stay home or go to church. Before I knew it, I ran back out of the house as fast as my legs could carry me.

As I arrived at my destination, I entered the church in my usual fashion by creeping in through the back door and sat at the back of the congregation as to go unnoticed. True to form, I arrived just at the end of worship to an introduction of the service which was for healing. Pastor Sarah explained that the purpose of the evening meeting was for any and everyone who needed to be

healed whether physical, emotional or mental. As I heard Pastor
Sarah speak in words of encouragement, inviting all those who
needed help to come forward, I toyed with the idea of asking for
healing of my shoulder, but again there was that voice trying to
talk me out of it and I heard the voice tell me not to say anything.
"There is no spiritual healing for you here" but the voice of Pastor
Sarah was louder as she continued praying over the congregation
with more power and authority, drowning out the other voice. I
can remember Pastor Sarah asking for people in the congregation
to identify themselves for healing by raising their hands and
even though I sat there in pain, I couldn't bring myself to do it.
I didn't feel confident to speak out and ask for help. I didn't feel
deserving or worthy. Part of me wasn't sure I even truly believed
in any form of healing power, but the pain I felt was leading me to
want to seek the help even if I wasn't sure that it actually worked.
Then a moment of clarity came. Pastor Sarah spoke out further
to say that she felt as if there was someone in the congregation
who was suffering with pain in their neck and shoulder and that
she encouraged them to speak out in their suffering. I gasped in
shock as I looked up and around to see if it was actually me that
the pastor was referring to. Suddenly, there was a shift inside of
me as I felt an urge and desire to put my arm up but just as I went
to do so, another woman had already placed her arm firmly in the
air confirming her as the right candidate. I reclined back into my
chair believing that Pastor Sarah's insight was not directed at or for
me, but that was not the end. Whilst Pastor Sarah acknowledged

the need of this other woman, she went on to say that she felt as if there was someone else in the congregation that was also suffering from a pain to the shoulder and neck and continued on to encourage them to identify themselves. Not only that, but she began to describe my exact symptoms and in that moment I knew she was talking directly about and to me. Before I could give it any more thought, the very same arm that was troubling me with the pain shot straight up in the air and before I knew it, I was walking towards the alter for healing prayer. I could not believe the steps I was taking; me who had always snuck in and sat at the back not wanting to engage was now taking very bold steps towards God. My path felt as if it were being swept clear with each step closer towards the front of the church. I couldn't understand what was going on but it didn't seem to matter as a very clear and evident peace and joy began sweeping over me. As I walked up the steps of the stage towards Pastor Sarah and stood in front of a huge congregation, I felt moved to tears. I had never in my life been so close to God and I could feel His presence beginning to fill my heart in a way that I had not experienced until that very moment and as Pastor Sarah laid her hands on me, I felt the touch of the Holy Spirit. It was as if there was heat rising through and out of my shoulder, and with it came a release. I could neither explain nor comprehend the feeling which passed through my body in that moment – it was powerful and it was freedom. It was as if the pain was extracted from my body, leaving behind a feeling of euphoria. After Pastor Sarah and the congregation had finished praying over me, I was asked how

my shoulder and neck felt. As I twisted my head from side to side,
rotating my arm, there was no more pain. I stood there, still circling
my arm with an expression of confusion over the disappearance of
the pain, but it had truthfully gone.

I literally stood there amazed at God's healing power.
I became emotional, but was thankful to Pastor Sarah and the
congregation for their intercessory prayer. As the tears flowed
down my face with a trembling in my voice, I went on to explain
of my struggles in accepting my journey to God. I explained that
I had always entered church feeling like a rejected sinner already
defeated, believing I had no real place amongst God's people or in
His heart. I went on to explain that I didn't believe in His healing
power over my life and that I had felt so lonely, but in that very
moment I wanted to acknowledge and openly give thanks to God
for His faithful and very evident love for me. It surpassed all of my
knowledge and I returned to my seat with a spring in my step and
a smile on my face. Later that evening, excitedly I told 'Everything'
about my encounter of God's healing power at church. It was the
first time I had ever felt as if I were a real part of a spiritual family
and a real connection to my spiritual home. I reflected on the
fact that at the beginning of the day I was in some kind of pain,
but it was evident that the pain I felt in my body was merely a
reflection of the pain in my mind. I acknowledged that up until
that day all of my bad choices including going to the bingo hall
were a means of and a way to block out that pain with some kind

of sinful distraction. Nevertheless God had continued to speak into my heart, despite the enemy's many attacks. He continued to try and work through and rescue me, and with that I realised God's intention was to reach into the very depths of my soul and love me from the inside out, bringing real life to my spirit. That day it felt as if God had taken me on a date, to the finest restaurant of faith to dine on the very best spiritual food His love could afford which was limitless. That day, God asked me what I wanted with no expense spared and He gave it to me right there and then. That very same day had started in place of spiritual void, but ended up in a place of victory. It was in that moment of being with God that a sense of real love was felt within me. The power of Jesus's love, his rescue and comfort was experienced on a deeper level and the power of God's grace took a hold of me. I felt butterflies in my stomach with the excitement of a brand new relationship. It felt as if God was that special guy…the new man in my life whom I eagerly waited in anticipation to hear from. He was the one whose calls I eagerly awaited. He was the one who I wanted to stay up late with, in all night communication. He was the one and my new promise to love. I didn't fully understand it, but I knew that something was changing….that I was changing.

CHAPTER 7

Baptism-Gate Part One

Waiting on and hearing from God had begun to feel easier. It was becoming habitual. Often during prayer I felt comfortable and confident in my time spent with The Father, and I could feel a real presence of the Holy Spirit as I grew in a better relationship with Him. I was beginning to know God much greater and learn of His ways and I could feel His will moving deeply in my heart with a true awakening and a fresh revelation. The bond felt stronger and I knew that I was developing a deeper level of understanding and a greater longing for God. I was beginning to feel confident in His love for me and that He was truly working through my circumstances to bring forth the desires of my heart. I began to really understand that to wait on God was to receive peace and the more I accepted and allowed Jesus into my life the more I allowed for my spiritual walk to transcend to another level. I was learning to rest in Him and it was like stepping out from the darkness into a very bright light. It was God who I believed was to be placed as priority in my life, with Him being the beginning and end of every day. As much as I loved 'Everything' I started feeling differently about who he was and where he should be placed in my life and, although I was still making some particularly bad choices which involved him, I knew that God still loved me and it was Him who was the one to change my life. I realised that only God could really change me from the inside out and make me better….make me whole. The thought of a different future excited me, and made me smile in a way that I had not ever experienced before, not even in my love for 'Everything'.

I began to feel alive in God's presence and for the very first time in my Christian walk, I knew with great sincerity that I had finally placed The Father in the centre of my heart and soul, with an ever growing desire to know Him more and more through Jesus. I wanted my life to reflect worship in Him. I wanted to live to serve Him and with that desire God had begun to move into His rightful place as my all rather than being the compromise He had always been; not only during my romantic relationship with 'Everything' but throughout my whole entire life. It had been a long time coming and finally it seemed as if something was happening within me. The desire inside felt stronger and was growing to an unshakeable faith that was most certainly becoming unbreakable.

God was moving. Finally I felt as if I had begun to feel stronger in the ability to conquer my fears and I began developing a confident spirit which yielded a belief that perhaps I could actually win my battles with Jesus by my side. Old demons and previous barriers were now being removed and my personal walls much like the walls of Jericho in the Book of Joshua. The walls that seemed so hard to defeat, seemed to fall away easily, almost like a feather delicately descending in the wind.

Something new and exciting was happening and I felt a fire for God in my growing desire to seek Him which came solely from my own longing to have a personal relationship with Him. Not only that, but it was becoming clearer that my breakthroughs were not happening by my own strength but because God and God alone made these happen by carrying me through and this was because of His great love for me. I had read in The Bible that God had spoken of His strength being made perfect in weakness; now I was becoming stronger through my trust and faith in Him. He was carrying me and so I felt an overwhelming desire to surrender. I wanted to be pleasing to My Father because I had felt a better understanding of His love, grace and mercy and in thanksgiving for what He had done for me; I wanted to begin in dedication of my life to Him through being baptised.

The decision was made, however it was no secret that in the past and during my relationship with 'Everything' I had been at that place of wanting to be baptised before and admittedly at the time it was for solely for 'Everything' and not really ever for God. Yes, I was attempting to be a better Christian by cementing further commitment by walking with Jesus, but this was blurred by a desire for the approval of 'Everything'. I believed that if I showed him how serious I was now in my faith – so much so that I was willing to accept Jesus as my Lord and Saviour through becoming baptised - it would then become inevitable for 'Everything' to then want more of me in his life. I believed that making an outward declaration would impress on his heart my greater value. I believed that he would of course have to love me more, respect me more and most importantly, see it all as confirmation that I was good enough to be his wife – a strong, God fearing woman full of love. I was wrong. Believing that I could trick him and use God was of great consequence and I was taught a strong lesson in discipline as my journey to being baptised was that of a very difficult one. The first time I put myself forward as a candidate to be baptised at my church 'Everything' fell ill and was admitted to hospital the very day before the baptismal ceremony was scheduled to take place. Something was found to be wrong with his heart and the illness came on with such great force…within a matter of hours. The whole experience placed such a fear in me. I was so afraid of losing him that I could not even bear the thought of going ahead with the baptism whilst he was so unwell, nor did I want to be baptised without him being there. 'Everything' had contributed greatly to my spiritual walk, and I had come to know and find God through his influence, so it was only right that I would postpone

until he was better and could be in attendance. I rationalised that
it was acceptable to forgo the baptismal ceremony believing that
God would understand my reasons for choosing not to go ahead.
Although I knew my place in God's heart had not changed or that
I had lost my place in Heaven by not being baptised at that time,
I was confessing an uncompromising love for a man when that
level of love should only have been for God. We all have free will
and I was afforded the opportunity, like all of God's children to
exercise mine, but as a woman who was trying to grow in Christ
I had put myself back by what felt like a thousand paces. The
growing sense of freedom in Christ that I had begun to experience
was now replaced with that all too familiar sense of bondage.
My relationship with God was no longer set upon a rock and
growing in strength as it had been doing and I began to feel guilty.
I was unsure of who I was and lacked direction again. I became
overwhelmed with false evidence appearing real believing that my
place in God's heart had changed. I also convinced myself that the
leaders of my church were disappointed and would now respond
differently towards me, but there was another aspect. It was
'Everything'. I convinced myself that he too was disappointed in me
and my choice to postpone the baptism. He had made it clear that
whilst he did not stand in judgement of my decision, he believed
that I should have continued with the baptism ceremony because it
was not about him but my journey with Jesus, and he was right. At
the time I was upset, offended and disappointed that 'Everything'
could not see the logic behind the sacrifice I had made – a choice

to wait because I had believed his inclusion in the process to be
of importance, and that if he was not a part of it I did not want to
continue. I was upset because he did not understand the depth; I
loved him and valued him that much – so much so, that I did not
want to do it without him, but as I began to digest his opinion it
forced me to confront my reasoning. The truth was that I had lost
sight of the fact that I had forgone the greater blessings of God.
I had traded in the gifting of baptism of the Holy Spirit through
accepting Jesus Christ for that of 'Everything'. I began to feel a
deeper sense of losing out, but I was also embarrassed that perhaps
I had made myself appear amateur in my understanding of what a
true relationship with God actually was and what it meant to be a
true follower of Christ. I had also done the exact opposite to what I
had intended to achieve and made myself appear less credible in the
eyes of 'Everything'. I anguished over the possibility that I had made
the wrong choice and with that, allowed myself to feel guilt and
condemnation. It was painful, and as the pain took a hold I grew
in a greater discomfort. I began to feel ashamed of not taking that
further step of commitment when I should have. I felt fraudulent
– as if my previous inner declaration of God being first in my life
was a lie and I had not been 100% honest of where He stood in my
heart. In truth, God had not been number one. Yes, He was steadily
and gradually moving into poll position but at the time I had first
decided to be baptised I had not truly placed Him in a position
where nothing else mattered. It was 'Everything' who still mattered
most in my heart and I had to firstly admit the imbalance in order

to make the necessary changes which placed The Father first and not an evident second.

I began working on my relationship with God again with a seemingly greater dedication, but I still struggled at best with fear and sin. I knew that whilst slowly but surely I was growing spiritually, there were things I continued doing which were not pleasing to God. I knew that He loved me, but there were still very evident compromises in my walk with Him. On occasion I would still share intimacy with 'Everything' and whilst it was not often, I knew that as an unmarried Christian couple we were indulging the flesh which created direct conflict with the spirit. Not only that, but there was a knowledge within me that the continued sin would block other blessings and any real spiritual revelations in both our lives. I knew that God could not and would not use us as He had intended whilst we continued in disobedience. He would not realise His purpose in our lives because He could not condone our actions. I knew that the sin would not only continue to hinder any growth, but would ultimately destroy our relationship with each other because it was not led by God or being nurtured with His blessing. The sin of sexual intimacy became a mist. It placed a veil of obscurity in place of a clear perspective. Ultimately I knew the consequences of my actions, but there were times where I would simply close my eyes and ignore the still whispering voice of God speaking to me. Instead of listening to Him, I would place my head upon the chest of 'Everything' and be comforted by the vibrations of his heartbeat rather than that of God. However, I knew that despite it all God still loved me and I believed that He understood my struggles and for that I was grateful. I knew that it was His loving grace and mercy which allowed me to come before Him time and time again to ask of His forgiveness, repent of my sins and get back on track. It was the growing knowledge of this unconditional love which transcended me from a place of conviction, to acceptance and change. I realised that whilst I understood earthly love through my relationship with 'Everything' there was an even greater supernatural love out there for me. It was a love so deep and one that was unfailing. It was a love that revealed so many layers and irrespective of how bad I was; no matter the mistakes, flaws or imperfections, I was loved every single day of my life. I could be confident that God, unlike other people and eventually even that of 'Everything', would never leave me. He would remain with me and by my side working with me to win. He wanted my life to be better – not just to look good, but to be good. My Father, God wanted a life for me that was limitless in His power and I began to understand it and accept that no matter what I did, HE would never forsake me. God loved me despite being a woman who had been faithless, who in the past had lacked in morals and blamed God for an unfortunate life when it became too difficult. Nevertheless it was becoming increasingly evident just how amazing and so very good God had always been to me, and I as grew in acceptance the guilt and condemnation began to disappear.

I began to work on renewing my mind. I made a choice to begin with small but consistent steps which involved correcting my thoughts to be in line with God's Word. It was very difficult for me as historically I had always overwhelmed my mind with negative thoughts and a belief system which centred on not thinking well of myself. I had always focused on my mistakes but now it was time to focus only on what God had to say about who I was and release any old belief systems that no longer served me. So I began again with prayer and devotional focus, but it was a constant challenge of distracting thoughts. There were times when I really did not feel encouraged because my mind would become overwhelmed with insecurities centred mostly on 'Everything', but I persevered in taking the appropriate action against the things of my mind which were hindering me. It was a process of taking steps to claim the right thoughts followed up with doing the right things (primarily by reading The Word of God), which then followed up with feeling the right things and a peacefulness in my soul that would allow for progress. Once I began to master this I noticed a return in my relationship with God moving back to its habitual and natural state. It was one that I had experienced before and the goodness of it was familiar. The presence of the Holy Spirit felt within reach and was tangible again. There was no longer that boundary between The Father and I. I was excited and began to sense God's Will once again growing in my heart, but even greater than before.

A growing number of months had passed, and I wanted God to show me a sign. I wanted confirmation from Him that it was finally the time for me to go to another level and move forward spiritually, so I asked the Holy Spirit to speak directly into my heart with an instruction. My desire to hear confirmation from Him meant being patient and trusting that He would answer at the appointed time. I had to diligently seek and wait, especially as I had previously failed at being a faithful servant in the past. It meant that waiting on His permission regarding baptism could only be engineered by my faith and so I found myself willing to wait on Him in the moment, remaining in a deeper place of patience until I heard the voice of God say yes. I had to wait patiently because I began to understand and readily accept that waiting on God saw the greatest benefit and reward. It meant that it was right in His timing and it came by His grace. Not only that, but I wanted to be completely led by the Holy Spirit, so that there would be no doubt in my heart where the instruction came from and I would be ready. I wanted to ensure that it wasn't just me coming up with a so called "good idea" in a moment during my Christian walk, or that I was being filled with worldly ambitions of the flesh. I wanted to focus solely on Jesus and this time I was going to get it right. I wasn't going to try and impress church leaders, friends, family or even 'Everything'…the only impression I wanted to carve out was a commitment to God through Jesus Christ and I wasn't going to complicate it. I continued to wait on God's yes with gentle requests through prayer to be baptised. I confessed being ready to fully accept Jesus and although I knew that My Father was not punishing me for my past mistakes, I knew that I would have to be disciplined by God in the same way as any father would his child he loves, and in my case it was through waiting. So I resigned myself to the possibility that I might have to wait some time, but remained focused on being ready. I asked God to give me a clear sign to show me when it might be time, giving an indication which left me without question or any doubt, and that sign came.

I sat one Sunday at church getting ready to hear the word. The Worship Team had just finished singing and the church leadership began reading out the weekly notices. As I sat there, I had not long bent my head down in quiet contemplation when I heard the pastor notify the congregation of an upcoming baptismal ceremony. Instantly I sat up like a meerkat with my eyes and ears fully switched on alert waiting to hear more. As the pastor continued to give the congregation further details on the baptismal classes available for potential candidates, the excitement and adrenalin had me moving around in my seat like an impatient child. I was itching to quickly place my hand in the air to show an interest in becoming a candidate. As I sat next to 'Everything' with a big cheesy grin on my face it seemed to confuse him, so I leant over to whisper an explanation and to express my joy at hearing confirmation that it was finally genuinely my time. As with anything that involved God, 'Everything' seemed happy and was supportive of going forward with baptism, so up went my hand as the pastor asked for those expressing an interest in baptism to identify themselves. I felt as if I had won the lottery. God had spoken to me and for the first time I knew that this was purely The Holy Spirit's guidance. I was happy. I was moving forward in my spiritual walk and in the next couple of months I would be there in an open declaration and acceptance of The Lord, Jesus Christ as my saviour. All I could think about was God's grace and I was thankful once again. I began to plan it all out in my mind, but then a sense of nervousness came over me as I thought about the reality of committing my life to Christ. Thoughts of not being ready, being undeserving and the question of whether or not I actually really and truthfully wanted to be baptised swamped my mind, but I knew that it was the enemy trying to confuse and fool me into believing his lies. I quickly recognised that he was trying to attack me in my mind where I had always struggled, but I found a way to ignore him and tune out. I was determined not to allow him in and began praying against the spiritual attack and it seemed to work. Satan was not getting through and as I felt him leave me alone, I relaxed and let the anxiety and doubt over my impending baptism disappear.

The following weeks seemed easy. It was as if life had finally started falling into place. My position at work changed for the better, family issues seemed less intrusive and 'Everything' and I were getting along well. There seemed to be progress in every aspect of my life as I moved closer to the run up of being baptised, and I knew that it was God blessing every part of the process. I soon forgot about the enemy and relaxed as I felt that God was supporting me, but in taking a more relaxed approach to life, I also took a more relaxed approach in my prayer life. In turn, less prayer meant I was spending less time with God. I found myself forgetting or was too tired to devote prayer time consistently. I became busy in my life and the distraction meant that I dropped my guard, leaving me open to the enemy. I began falling into sporadic prayer and devotional time, and began leaning on myself and 'Everything' that bit more rather than on God. Whilst I was aware of the fact I had become less apt, I didn't feel a sense of worry or fret because I focused my thoughts and rescue to the impending baptism. I felt confident that all would be alright but things slowly began to fray around the edges of my life ever so subtly.

The first question mark came when I was contacted by an older friend from my church asking if I were free to meet and have coffee with an elder and his wife. Her evasiveness over the purpose of the meeting left me questioning why and so very out of the blue I had been asked to attend urgently. I was happy to do so, but when I was asked to meet them without the presence of 'Everything', who should have been involved as my life partner, set off alarm bells. Quickly, I ascertained that it was in relation to my current living situation. 'Everything' and I were living together and not separately as we should have been as an unmarried Christian couple and so we were living in sin. As I was approached by my older friend, it wasn't referred to quite in the context of sin, but it was deemed as 'inappropriate.' As a result, it put a question mark over whether or not I should be baptised and as elders and friends indirectly attempted to assist in facilitating a temporary separation in the living arrangements, 'Everything' and I continued to press on under the one roof. Nonetheless, the pressure to change the living arrangements continued as that same older friend expressed that being baptised whilst living with a man and being unmarried was not right. I became emotional and upset, and considered withdrawing from my place as a candidate. I was confused. I wanted to do the right thing by withdrawing if my conduct set an inappropriate example, but at the same time I did not want a repeat of what had happened during my previous attempt of baptism; I did not want to be full of regret that I did not put Jesus first. All I had wanted to do was move closer to God through a deeper acceptance of Him by demonstrating an outward expression of showing my love for Him. I did not know what to do and so instead of consulting with God, I went to 'Everything'. I had always valued his opinion but seeking his counsel instead of God meant that I tripped up once again by leaving God out of the process. This was my first mistake.

As I anguished over what to do with tears of sadness, I waited on the response of 'Everything'. I believed that he would know what the right thing to do was. During our discussion and my explanation of events, I confessed to 'Everything' that I believed I should withdraw from baptism. I wanted to do the right thing, but all the lines were blurred and I was beyond the point of knowing what to do. Emotionally and spiritually I was exhausted. I was tired of the apparent judgement over my relationship with 'Everything'. As far as I was concerned, we had always tried our best, with limited resources, to do the right thing whilst serving God. I was upset that our church stood in judgement of our living situation without knowing how or why we lived together. We both had limited resources, but wanted to work towards a future together. Admittedly, we both accepted that it was not ideal as a Christian couple, but when I moved into the home with 'Everything' sometime before, I had not accepted Jesus into my life and was solely focused my own selfish needs. Back then 'Everything' and I had just got together and had big plans for the future, so living together seemed logical as it would allow for those plans to become realised. In my mind, moving into his home meant that I (we) could save up and putting our resources together creating better opportunities. I had not moved into his home knowing that it would be sinful or that later it would impact on the validity of my spiritual standing. I had moved in solely with the purpose to make our lives better, but somehow my careless decision in a moment of innocence had in-turn become a major problem which had to be addressed and we could not remain as we were.

'Everything' was adamant that I should not withdraw as a candidate for baptism and his opinion was that my journey was always to be about God and me, nothing or no-one else. I loved that he seemed to be on my side and understood the real purpose, which was my salvation and being reborn in Christ. He never saw himself in any part of it and he simply did not see himself as important enough to be considered and I admired that in him.

'Everything' just wanted to help facilitate the process of smoothly getting me to where I needed to be spiritually and so after a lengthy discussion, he suggested that he move out of our room and that moving forward we were to sleep in separate spaces apart from each other. As I resisted the idea with more tears and panic, he reassured me that it would all be okay and that we had to do what was pleasing to God. The idea of separating filled me with panic; I didn't like the idea of sleeping in separate places not for one single second, but I had to agree that we needed to bite the bullet and put God first. This was not like it was in the beginning where we did not know better – we had both actively grown as Christians who desired more of God's presence in our daily lives and so we had to make an outward declaration and choices that reflected our belief. That very same night I slept alone in our bed as 'Everything' moved to the room next door. I was filled with a fear over the very distinct possibility of our romantic relationship changing to a platonic one. We had already made a decision to no longer share intimacy in our dedication to please God, and had done so even before the issue surrounding our living together had been established. I felt that the separation would make it impossible to stay "in love" if we no longer even shared the same bed and I became convinced that the new sleeping arrangements would catapult us into becoming like flatmates. I was adamant that I did not want the impending transition to happen because I loved 'Everything' and I wanted him to remain in love with me, but despite the difficulty, I tried to release the thoughts that were swimming around in my head and trust that if we were faithful to God in this, then in turn He would be faithful to us and cement our relationship despite the growing difficulties stacked up against it. I lay there thinking about them both; the two most important elements of my life being God and 'Everything' and in that moment, I determined myself to love them with all of my heart with an even deeper commitment to succeed than ever before. Despite at varying times it being difficult to love them, I was so happy that I had found God and 'Everything' and so very grateful for being blessed by their acceptance of me. As I thought more about my two great loves, I felt a sense of relief come over me in the decision that 'Everything' and I had made to separate, and I felt a growing confidence that it was the right thing to do. I believed with great conviction that My Father would readily accept me with open arms and approve of the new living arrangements – after all, 'Everything' and I had cut all ties that made our living together inappropriate and without any further pitfalls, it was time to fully receive Jesus.

However, Satan had not finished his work yet.

CHAPTER 8

Baptism-Gate Part Two

I pressed on with preparing for the day of my baptism. I was
determined to have a mind cleared of any thoughts or distractions
that took away my focus, so I kept busy by throwing myself in to
God's word and began a New Believers course at church. As the
weeks went by and the run up to the baptism ceremony turned
into being only a matter of days away, I pondered thoughts about
my dedication to Jesus. I wasn't doubtful but I was mindful of
impending changes, so I prayed to God for him to strengthen my
walk even further, to clear away any emotional debris and for Him
to prepare me so that I was best ready to accept Jesus Christ into
my life. As I felt His strength and righteousness come over me, I felt
more solid in my convictions and a real sharpening in my spirit,

but I also pondered the idea of being tested. I had read various stories in The Bible of testing and I was convinced that my faith would be stretched in a capacity of some sort through a trial of my own faith, and so as I continued in my devotional time with God I also prayed for Him to reveal any pitfalls that I may have been heading towards. With my request made to The Father, I waited and watched, remaining in awareness.

The morning of my baptismal ceremony I woke up in a state of peace and with a firm sense of readiness about me. Although previously the starting line had yielded a stumbling out of the racing blocks of my spiritual life, somehow I had managed to pick myself back up and continue on to a place where I could then see the finishing line. I already felt like a winner, as I imagined myself running comfortably into the arms of Jesus who was there waiting for me welcomingly. Things had finally reached a turning point from the earlier days of my life. In the beginning, my journey had seen one of a broken and bitter young woman. I had never known what true love was until finally, I had decided to give God a small window of chance to work amidst the chaos I had created when he blessed me with the introduction of 'Everything'. God took me and my mess; a work in need of much progress and with the help of a passionate Christian man, peeled away the many damaged layers to open up my heart to His love. Not only that, but I knew God had not even nearly begun to reveal the capacity of His intentions for my life and all that He planned to give me. I hadn't done anything to deserve His gifting but it didn't matter because He had chosen me for a role that only I could fulfil. I learnt to accept through the many church meetings and leadership teaching that before I was born God had begun moulding me for His purpose to make a difference in the world and that we are all moulded for a unique purpose. It was all by His Grace. l didn't need to question how God would use me or why he thought I could possibly do anything at all of any use, but I was to continue in a place of simply just accepting His unfailing love through my dedication and nothing was going to hold me back.

Later that morning, I went to the usual 11.15am service at church with 'Everything' and enjoyed the powerful time of praise and worship, but this time it felt different as I acknowledged within myself that it was to be the last one before I would be giving my life to Christ. The excitement continued to grow throughout the day as the hours grew closer to the evening baptismal service. In a pre-celebratory lunch, 'Everything' and I laughed and joked in a time of fellowship with some friends at our favourite café, but the mood quickly changed when I noticed a voicemail alert pop up on my mobile phone. It was a message from Elder Alan of our church, who was part of the leadership team. As I listened carefully to the message instructing me to make contact with him regarding my baptism, a sudden feeling of nervousness and apprehension overcame me. As I finished listening to the message it was obvious to everyone at lunch that something had happened as my facial expression and body language shifted. As 'Everything' asked me what was wrong, I proceeded to give him and the others details of the message I had just listened to. I expressed concern over what Elder Alan might have wanted to speak to me about and was convinced that it was about my actual baptism. "They're not going to let me do it are they?" were the words that fearfully came out of my mouth, but 'Everything' was convinced that it was not relating to my baptism specifically and confidently expressed his belief that the message must have been concerning another matter. Usually his level headed rationality would automatically calm me, but this time it did not work and I began to feel an increased sense of unrest and pensiveness. We continued on with our lunch, but whilst the others laughed and chattered away, I could think of nothing else but the message and as heightened paranoia set in, I quickly lost my appetite. I was scared. My intuition told me something was not right, but rather than debate it in my mind I decided to pluck up the courage and return the call. I excused myself from the dining table in the café and went back to my car. As I sat in the driver's seat I felt nowhere near in control of my emotions. I took a deep breath, closed my eyes and paused before returning the call. As I pressed dial and waited for the call connection, the silence became deafening as I wanted to hang up, but just in that very moment Elder Alan who had left the earlier message answered. We exchanged polite greetings and asked how each other were and for a brief moment I breathed a sigh of relief as the tone of the conversation didn't appear formal. It seemed that once again 'Everything' had been right and that it wasn't anything for me to worry about but then the purpose of Elder Alan's call was revealed.

"Can you come to have a meeting with me before the baptismal ceremony?" he asked. I was confused. Why did he want to meet with me right before the baptismal ceremony? My tone shifted to one of questioning and I asked for greater indication of the purpose of meeting earlier. It seemed that Elder Alan did not want to disclose why he had wanted to meet with me over the phone, but I was already too nervous to wait another minute to find out what he wanted. At this point I had guessed the obvious. I knew that he wanted to meet with me to tell me the inevitable…that my baptism would not be going ahead, but I wasn't prepared to go to church ready to be baptised with friends and family in tow only to be told it wasn't going ahead. With a direct but polite tone I made a request. "If it is okay with you, I would prefer if you told me now what is going on," were my words to him. By now I was trembling in anticipation of what was to come next, and as my eyes began to fill up with tears Elder Alan delivered the instruction from church leadership that I was to be withdrawn as a candidate from the baptismal ceremony.

Nothing prepared me for that sinking feeling and I burst into tears as I listened to the reasons as to why I had been removed as a candidate, and as sure as the sun rises every day, it was because I was living as an unmarried Christian with 'Everything'. The church felt that to proceed would have not set a good example to the youth of the congregation (amongst others in the church) if I were to be baptised whilst remaining in a living situation which the church leadership did not agree with. Whilst I understood their view point, in a last ditched attempt to reason with Elder Alan and perhaps change their minds I explained my position. I explained that initially when I moved in with 'Everything' I was not then a born again believer and did not have an understanding of the principles behind a man and woman living together unmarried and how this might have affected their spiritual standing. I went on to explain that 'Everything' and I had not shared intimacy nor had we slept in the same bed for a very long time, particularly since we both became more serious in our faith and spiritual standing. I then went on to explain, somewhat in desperation, that we had even changed our living arrangements so that we were not even sharing the same room! I begged and pleaded in an attempt to show some sort of willing and change in my mind-set. I even expressed that I felt it was somewhat unfair that I was being penalised for a decision that was beyond my control because I had always wanted to get married, however it was clear that 'Everything' was not ready to marry me and obviously the decision had to be that of a joint one. I even went on further to explain my sadness and feelings of refection at not being asked by 'Everything' to marry him as I would have readily accepted, but still the answer was the same. It was no. As Elder Alan went on to explain in greater depth the church viewpoint, he explained that the decision was not to punish or hurt me, but to support my further growth. The church wanted to encourage me to take the necessary steps and make changes spiritually which included a number of things, but the overall viewpoint was that I strongly needed to change my living arrangements. I was not angry at first, but once again I felt rejected and confused. I couldn't understand why I could not be accepted by God because I lived with a man that I loved and intended as my husband if only he would have me. I felt as if the decision had been made without my consent and an opportunity for my salvation had been ripped away from me without a justifiable reason...not in my mind. I sat there on the other end of the phone, hanging on for dear life. I tried to obtain a change in viewpoint from the elder, but the decision was final and there was no possible way that the church was going to accept my situation and allow my baptism to go ahead on that day. As I continued to sob heartfelt tears over the phone, Elder Alan tried to encourage me to see it as a necessary position to help me in the long run. He also left me with a thought; to see the changes through as he believed that they would mark an even more powerful testimony in my spiritual walk and to not let go of the changes for a better future.

Not long after his final words, the call ended and I was alone. I continued to sit in the car and cry. I was inconsolable as I tried to digest what had just happened, replaying his last words over and over again. I did not know what to do or what it all meant in terms of my spiritual standing. I questioned if I would still be accepted as a member of the church or if it meant I too was excluded from the congregation. I questioned if it meant I would never have the opportunity to be baptised at my church or anywhere else, but the biggest question was over who I was in Christ at that moment in time. I also questioned God's presence in a moment of loneliness. Whist I sat there, eyes filled with tears so much so that my vision was blurred, suddenly that all too familiar tall figure stood outside my car. 'Everything' had come to check on me; I had been missing from the lunch table for a while and he wanted to know if I was okay. As I looked at him, he knew the reason for my tears. There wasn't much to say but I could see that he was disappointed on my behalf as I briefly explained the conversation with Elder Alan. As we excused ourselves from the remainder of the lunch, 'Everything' drove me home and once I got to the house, the remainder of my cooped up emotions exploded as I collapsed into a heap of inconsolable tears. For a while, I couldn't stop crying. Even as I washed dishes and tidied up around me as a means of distraction, I could not stop the tears. 'Everything' was also hurt by my growing sadness and I could see from his own confused expression that he may have felt some degree of responsibility. 'Everything' wanted answers and wasn't willing to just accept the reasoning of the church viewpoint and wanted to speak with Elder Alan over the decision. I pleaded with him to let it go, but the whole situation had become bigger than just my exclusion. He wanted to know for his own spiritual understanding why the church had made this decision as it placed him in confusion and he expressed that their reasoning had come into conflict with all that he had known in his seven years as a Christian. 'Everything' wanted answers and insisted on seeking them. It upset me even more to see him so angry on my behalf with those who he had come to call his spiritual family – those who had plucked him from obscurity and brought him to Christ. I felt that I had already caused too much controversy and at this stage, wanted only to climb under a rock and hide away in my pain as I had always done before. I tried desperately to let it go, but found myself unable to gain any real control over my emotions for any length of time during the remainder of the evening. When I paused long enough and thought deeper into the events of the day, I felt overcome with grief over my failings. Once again I had let God down with my poor choices and ultimately it came down to a decision over my relationship with 'Everything'. I was faced with the very evident need of making a decision concerning the future of my relationship with God verses my relationship with 'Everything'. It was now laid out with no illusions that a choice had to be made. I couldn't continue on as I had been and it was evident that 'Everything' was no longer able to remain the driving parameter and platform which God had initially used in an attempt to enter into my life. He would have to be placed elsewhere whilst God took His rightful lead. There had to be a sacrifice for the greater good of God's intentions in my life, but whatever needed to be done, the decision had to be made solely by myself. I would have to choose.

My mind reflected on both God and 'Everything' as I visualised both of them and their meaning in my life. I loved God; with all that I had, I gave him the best of me, but 'Everything' still had the depths of my heart. In that moment I realised why the events of the day had happened with my baptism once again not taking place....it was because I still placed 'Everything' before

God. I questioned what was I doing and how I could have allowed myself to end up in the very same place as before. The truth was that I was never going to move beyond the very spot I stood at in my relationship with God because of the continued compromise. If I wasn't ever going to fully commit to placing God as my Alpha and Omega, acknowledging His existence in my life as priority and to truly nurture my relationship with Him, I would fail. If I continued to place Him as an afterthought once I had looked after the needs of 'Everything', I was going to see a disastrous season fall upon my life in the form of the one thing I would never give up and that was to be my relationship with 'Everything'. Exhausted and emotionally challenged beyond my capability, I wasn't willing to deal with any more than I could in that very moment. I was again beaten. Just when I thought I had made it through to a better place in my life I was cut down. In that very moment of defeat, all I wanted to do was sleep to escape it all. I paused in my brokenness and for a moment I felt the presence of The Holy Spirit. The Father had sent me a comforter but instead of accepting and allowing the comfort to enter in, I chose to ignore it. Instead, I reminded myself of an earlier conversation in prayer where I had asked God to help prepare and strengthen me for what was to come. I pondered over the possibility of missing the warning signs of my testing or perhaps I had simply ignored them because they centred on my 'Everything', but I could no longer ignore God's voice. The voice I had waited to hear from for so long had finally spoken but it was not as expected. Away from all of the noise of life and Satan's lies,

I could hear the instructions and warning signs clearly but still I did not want to give him up. I didn't know how to let 'Everything' go even if it meant forsaking my relationship with God. How would I give up the one thing I had asked God for my whole entire life? How would I give up on the one person responsible for my survival? How would give up on love?

My test had only just begun.

CHAPTER 9

Flying the Nest

It was becoming increasingly obvious that life was reverting back to a place of difficulty between us and things were not right in our relationship. 'Everything' and I continued on with everyday life trying to place the events of the baptism behind us. We tried to act as normal as possible, but it was evident that we both had a question mark over living together when it was confirmed that we should not be. However there was no discussion about it and between us as we both seemed to bury our heads in the sand, try to keep calm and carry on. We pressed on with our separate living arrangements: me sleeping in our bedroom whilst he remained in the room next door. Each day we would carry out our usual routines both individually and together, but at night we would say our goodnights and go to our respective rooms. I began noticing that we had started to adopt what I felt were bad habits in our demonstration of affection toward each other; forgetting to greet one another with a good morning kiss or the giving of a loving cuddle as we would say our goodnights – and although it was very evident that there was a dismissal of this normal act of affection or emotional acknowledgement, I remained silent. I couldn't bring myself to say anything to 'Everything' because I was no longer sure within myself what was right or deemed acceptable. I was also no longer sure of how 'Everything' actually still felt about me and with each day passing, there was a growing sense of fear building up inside me as I watched him become more distant. Not only that, there were decisions that needed to be made about our living situation and a very evident growing sense of God's voice of instruction that we should separate. I was overwhelmed and in turmoil over what I should do. I felt as if time was running out, as if I was literally watching the sand disappear through the egg timer of my relationship. I wanted to do what was right and leave the home to go it alone, but my heart was still with 'Everything'. I did not want to leave him. I felt that if I walked away from our home to live alone, I too would be walking away from our relationship which I wasn't ready to do. There was also a lack of confidence within me that our relationship could survive if we were not living together. I didn't understand that in actual fact, the only way for us to survive at the time as a couple was to walk away from a situation that was causing us both to hit a brick wall in our spiritual walk with Christ.

Once again I was confused, but I didn't quite know how to put the situation to God in prayer. Instead I remained in a state of emotional imbalance upset about most things, but particularly the events surrounding my failed baptism. I felt that amongst the difficulties surrounding my relationship with 'Everything' I was left with unanswered questions and residual feelings. I wasn't able to concentrate or focus; I felt disappointed and lonely. I no longer had a place of sanctuary in God where I could lay down my burdens and I missed that special place of peace. However, the feeling of disappointment kept me in a growing place of resentment, which I seemed unable to get rid of. I knew that I had to continue on in my journey with God, heeding His instruction and pressing through the struggles by continuing to pray faithfully. I knew that I had to press on and continue with going to church and with seeking to develop my relationship with Christ, but I no longer felt a growing desire to really try as I previously had. I felt weary, drained and afraid. I knew I was losing sense of control, but instead of leaning on God I buried my head in the sand.

Despite the struggles, the one person that seemed to keep me going was 'Everything'. My motivation to see it all through to completion came as direct result of my desire to please him and be with him. I believed that if I wanted to succeed in winning his love, enough so that he would ask me to be his wife, I knew that I would have to dig even deeper in my faith. However, instead of acknowledging in that very moment, that the appropriate action was to walk away from a spiritually toxic living situation even if for a short period of time, I remained. Things quickly deteriorated going from bad to worse between 'Everything' and I with what seemed like an ongoing battle in understanding each other's needs and who we were as individuals. It seemed that the more I dug my heels in holding on, the more distant 'Everything' seemed almost as if he wanted to escape. I literally watched before my very eyes, a man who once had a determined spirit to see us succeed, turn to one who just passively sat back and watched our relationship go by. It was obvious that we were both affected by the impact of the failed baptism and the discord seemed evident in both our behaviours; he became more distant while I grew in my resentment.

In my growing struggles, I stopped going to church. I couldn't face seeing everyone and having to answer questions over the baptism, so I remained away from any real Christian fellowship for a growing number of weeks. Eventually I plucked up enough courage to return to church. It was more of a decision rather than a feeling, as I still felt wretched and lost. I can remember walking through the doors with 'Everything' and Sonia and feeling as if all eyes were on me from the congregation and church leadership alike. As I stood up through worship trying to lift my voice towards The Lord, all I could focus on were distracting thoughts of no longer belonging. I felt weak and as if I couldn't stand up. I sat back down to recover the feeling, but nothing seemed to work. All I wanted to do was get out of there, but I knew that I had to be at church...I needed to be. So I fought against the feelings and remained for as long as I could, but it wasn't long before I felt completely suffocated by my surroundings and as if I couldn't breathe. I began to feel light headed as I tried to focus on fighting for air, and continuing on in what felt like a battle to stay and receive peace from the Holy Spirit. Tears began to well up, as I desperately tried to conceal them by closing my eyes to prevent my tears from falling. In that very moment, I felt as though I could no longer stay there and so I picked up my belongings as fast as I could and left in an attempt to get away without being seen in floods of tears.

As I returned to my car and sat there, I felt confused but mostly overwhelmed with sadness. I felt as if I was being completely stripped of all control over my life and of the things I desperately wanted without any real explanation. I felt a sense of being punished over what I believed was not my fault, but mostly I was perplexed by the heightened sense of pain in my mind, heart and spirit. I felt anguish over my belief that the church had rejected me, and I felt that 'Everything' truly did not want me or see me as good enough to be his wife. It seemed that despite whatever I had tried to do in a demonstration of my love and commitment to him, it was not enough and it hurt. I sat there in the car with tears streaming down my face questioning God over why my walk with Him was revealing what felt like a real sense of suffering and why it was not the seemingly joyful and peaceful journey as promised. It had seemingly not revealed the blessings in abundance given in a commitment to Him through Jesus Christ and I felt that I had been dealt a bad hand in a card game of the Christian life. I felt that I had been led into a false sense of security, believing that all would have worked out instead of feeling alone. I sat there in what felt like a debate with God over why he was being so hard on me when all I had wanted to do was try and love Him the best I could, become a wife and eventually a mother. I didn't have an expectation of big gestures from either The Father or 'Everything'; I just wanted to be loved and accepted by both, but it felt as if I was being told no. I didn't understand.

I continued to sit there with eyes closed in quiet contemplation when I heard voices approaching the car. I looked up to see it was 'Everything' and Sonia. As they got inside, I quickly tried to gather myself together and with an apology for disturbing their worship time, I explained what had happened and how I was feeling. Both 'Everything' and Sonia listened carefully as I expressed openly all of the hurt I was experiencing. As I talked through my sadness with a broken voice and tears, 'Everything' sat back quietly as Sonia held my hand to try and comfort me. I talked over my sadness at feeling as though he did not deem me good enough to be his wife and also how the lack of progress in our relationship left me feeling rejected. As I continued to talk and cry 'Everything' remained silent. It wasn't that he was unsympathetic, but he remained neutral and unmoved by my plea for answers. It seemed as if he made a deliberate choice to remain still giving very little in response and that day of confessing my pain to both him and God forged no concrete answers for me.

Things eventually came to a head when a family dispute meant that it was time for me to leave the home in which I had shared with 'Everything'. It came at a time when I had wanted to make the steps to leave but still wasn't brave enough to do so, and now I had no choice. At the time I did not realise that there was a warning and a lesson to learn from God. More to the point, that there was an obvious guiding from the Holy Spirit to make a right choice where the living arrangements were concerned. It was time for me to move on to a new home without 'Everything' and into a brave new chapter in which The Father would be well pleased, but still I couldn't quite see the vision. I wanted the change as I knew it had to happen and was one which I needed, but I still wanted 'Everything' more. There was something inside me which would not accept God's instruction. I reflected on previous words of advice from church leadership over the importance of changing the living situation and as the words ran over and over in my mind I tried to ignore them, but they were very clear. Nothing was going to progress for the better until I made the necessary changes which placed God first before anything else. The church leadership had reinforced the importance of living apart from 'Everything' – that was the reason for my removal as a baptism candidate, yet there I was still in doubt of the instruction. I was ignoring the very obvious warning signs to break away from the bondage which was stopping God to move in my life and relationship with 'Everything'. The problem was an issue of trust; trusting in God through all things and trusting in 'Everything' that he would remain with me as promised. I just couldn't seem to surrender to God's will and allow my faith to take charge rather than my emotions. I knew that God had placed before me a choice to exercise my freewill, but He had also previously demonstrated the consequences of my deliberate disobedience through the failed baptism. Still I put a question mark over it, convincing myself that perhaps my reflection of such things was of a direct result of my overthinking and nothing else, but I was wrong. It was a clear direction from the Holy Spirit.

During the time of family dispute, it was clear that the situation was affecting 'Everything' and eventually he confirmed that he was unhappy with a few things including our relationship. As I listened to him talk openly about his feelings, I convinced myself that his words were confirmation that unless I did something drastically to fix our relationship that it would soon be over. I believed that I had to do something and that walking away to go and live apart from him was not the answer, especially as it seemed that there was an obvious stumbling block with us moving closer together in a deeper commitment to each other. I convinced myself in that very moment and more so than ever, I had to take care of 'Everything' and fix us. I had to salvage the wreckage quickly and effectively. In that moment I ignored what God may have wanted or had planned for our lives and moved on to my own plan of action. As we talked over potential ideas to move forward,

I went into survival mode throwing anything I could into the mix of conversation which brought him round to my way of thinking. I could tell from the conversation that 'Everything' was unsure about our relationship and was in some conflict about whether or not he wanted it to end. I knew at this point he still loved me, but the love was diluted by doubt. He seemed worn down by the struggles and wanted a change. I too wanted a change and was in agreement there, but I did not want that change to be an end to me and him. So I continued on in suggesting a plan of a fresh start for both of us by moving into a new home together on our own as opposed to living in his family home which we shared with one of his parents and another sibling, which I believed had been a big part of the problem for us in our relationship. But the truth was, the family home was not the problem and moving into a new place was certainly not the solution. As I continued on in putting my case forward to 'Everything' over why I thought it was such a good idea to move in together to a new place, I could tell there was still an air of uncertainty surrounding the conversation. Although he seemed positive about the idea of a new home, it was evident there was still something unsettling to him. More to the point, there was an unsettling in my own spirit. I knew that the decision to move into a new home with 'Everything' was wrong and would yield no good fruit. I knew that my choice was a direct act of disobedience and I would have to learn a valuable lesson, but in that moment I felt that I had no choice. As I sat with 'Everything' laptop in hand looking at property websites, I reflected deeper on what I had just done. I had been told time and time again by some close friends and by church leadership that I needed to act in accordance with God's will by living separately from 'Everything' yet still I ignored it. I reflected further on that all important conversation I previously had with Elder Alan on the day of my failed baptism. I had passionately pleaded my case, explaining that I had not previously understood the spiritual implications of living as part of an unmarried Christian couple, but what could excuse my present actions? How could I ask for favour from God in blessings with a fruitful relationship when I was continuing to turn away from God, ignore Him and not place Him at the centre of my life? It was clear that I knew better and that what I was doing was wrong.

God had given me a choice. Time and time again, The Father had given me an opportunity to change things by placing very obvious warning signs in front of me and, by trying to, help me avoid the impending destruction which was to be the end of my relationship with 'Everything'. I had previously made a promise to love God and wanted to make that outward declaration in commitment of love through baptism, but I was told that I needed to change my priorities by placing Him first before 'Everything'. Not only that, I had also been prompted by the Holy Spirit to make those changes, so the instruction was clear. A part of those changes was also a testing of my faith and the truth of what was really in my heart, but also to strengthen me as a woman in Christ and to take me to the next level in my walk with God. To know and understand His heart and His ways could only come through trust and that was what God was asking me to do; to trust and obey Him, but I still could not elevate my mind above lower level thinking. I could not see that what I was saying had to be a true reflection of what I actually believed and wanted for my life. I had said that I truly wanted God in my life as priority, but there I was sitting with 'Everything' looking for a new place for us to live. It was as if I was laughing at and mocking God's instruction, and although it was never my intention to act in a way displeasing to God or demonstrating that I did not fear His instruction, I was falling into a trap of doing just that.

I was stuck. Thoughts kept circling my mind that it was a bad idea, but I continued on with 'Everything' looking on the internet at property sites for a place to live. As I turned and looked at him for approval, I felt consumed with love and in the haziness of bad choices, his face comforted me and convinced me that what I was doing was right. I tried to reconcile in my mind that such a strong powerful feeling of love had to have come from God and that He had not placed 'Everything' and I together for us simply to go our separate ways. I convinced myself that God would forgive me and make a way for us even through our situation. I rationalised that God knew I was a trying servant, and in my trying would say that it was fine for us continue living under the same roof. Deep down in my heart I knew it was not fine, but I was torn between my love for The Father and my greater love for 'Everything'. I felt ashamed that deep inside my heart, my love was compromised for

God and not as it should have been, but I pressed on with plans to move forward with 'Everything'.

We quickly found a new place to live. Our search for a new home seemed effortless, as we secured a nice one bedroom apartment. It had all we needed. It had a great amount of space at an affordable price and was in the perfect location for us. We both felt happy and eager to move into our new home and I for one saw it as the brand new start we needed. The new place felt like a blank canvas, and one that was going to allow us the freedom to paint a very beautiful picture of our future. We did all the usual things a couple do when moving into a new home together, buying furniture and crockery to create our own personalised space. I had wanted to make a real home for us both, but mostly I wanted 'Everything' to feel as though he had his own home which he controlled, but soon enough I was the one deciding on how and where things should go and how they should be. 'Everything' being who he was, calmly sat back and allowed me to have what I wanted. He had always allowed me to have my way – I believe it was always a part of his gentle and easy going character to just let me have things mostly my way as he didn't like stressful situations. However there were times when I mistook his passiveness for laziness and often I would berate him for his seemingly laid back approach to getting things done. I couldn't see that I was not only taking charge, but taking over. I was failing to take a step back allowing 'Everything' to be the integral part of the new process. In addition,

I had placed God on the side lines and dampened His voice much the same way I had done with 'Everything'. He was always there as I still believed, but I had compartmentalised Him in an attempt to forget about my disobedience. I knew that both 'Everything' and I were both equally responsible for our choices, but I felt a growing sense of responsibility over the situation because I had been the one to really facilitate the move to the new home. I continued on ignoring the niggling feeling inside of me, but it felt as if it were the Holy Spirit reminding me that I still had to make the choice to change my perspective. It was clear that He was not going to go away until the right choices were made but I continued to run away from His voice.

CHAPTER 10

The Beginning of the End

Within the first couple of weeks of moving into the new place saw our first major stumbling block. A few months prior to the big move, I began developing a growing sense of insecurity in the relationship as we became less emotionally attached to one another. I began looking for vital hints or clues as to why 'Everything' seemed to be changing in his feelings towards me. In the early part of our relationship I had never checked up on 'Everything' or invaded his privacy as I was confident in his feelings towards me and I trusted him in all things, because he had never given me reason to think otherwise. Nevertheless there was a growing change and during that change saw an increasing concern within me. I started out looking at the odd text message here and there which grew in consistency the less confident I became. I didn't want to check up on 'Everything' but in checking I always hoped I would never find anything. For the most part there wasn't really anything to write home about, but on a particular day where I had checked his phone it revealed something I was not comfortable with. There was a message in exchange of conversation with an ex-girlfriend and whilst she was just that, I knew her to be an ex of significance. She was the one girl who 'Everything' remained close with and was the one woman who caused him to have a question mark over being with me when we first met. She was the ex who made me feel inferior and insecure. She was the one who I believed was still somewhere in his heart and seeing her name on the message history scared me, manifesting unreasonable fear and paranoia. As I took a deep breath and read through the exchange of conversation, it revealed what I believed a tone of reminiscence and it hurt. It seemed as if 'Everything' missed her and not only that, he wanted her to know as such. In truth there was nothing to suggest dishonesty, but a longing for something else in him and that made the exchange of messages significant. Initially I wasn't sure what I should do. After all, I should not have been snooping around in his phone to reveal anything in the first place, but I couldn't ignore it and so I approached 'Everything' for answers. At first he seemed dismissive of my questioning over their contact, but his attitude quickly changed to one of wanting to reassure me that whilst he acknowledged that it was an inappropriate exchange, he truly loved me and that it was only me which he held romantically in his heart.

He further went on to say that he would cease contact with the ex in a bid to prove how important I was in his life and that he did not want to lose me, but at the same time he wanted me to understand that our relationship would not be able to work without trust.

There is was…that word 'trust.' It was something I had always struggled with in my relationship with God but now it was playing out with 'Everything'. Whilst he was right, I could already tell that my insecurities were getting the better of me as I felt an overwhelming need to dig deeper into his privacy by checking other things. My search was not to check up on him as such, but a bid to establish concrete reassurance for me that nothing was going on. Looking into things wasn't difficult to do as both 'Everything' and I had always shared passwords to various things including social network logins and our phone passcodes so it was easy to search for clues and subsequent answers, but every time I went on my detective hunt, I never found anything of any real significance. I hated that I was checking up on him and becoming untrustworthy myself, but couldn't resist the urge as I felt my relationship slipping further and further away. A growing sense of insecurity in our relationship began to overwhelm me and in an attempt to gain some reassurance, I began consulting with close friends. It was suggested that perhaps whilst he still loved me, he might no longer have been in love with me and although I knew that all opinions were said to help me move forward and with love, I was broken by the possibility that 'Everything' no longer felt the same way about me. I began thinking about the future and if there truly was one for the both of us together. We had previously spoken about marriage and children, but after a number of years into our relationship we were no closer to making any firmer commitments. It seemed obvious to me why that may have been the case; with the reminiscent text messages to the ex, coupled with the shift in our relationship confirmed that 'Everything' did not want to take things any further with me. The truth was that whilst it hurt, the apparent truth was no surprise to me at all. I had known it for some while as it had been stirring in the pipelines. I had guessed it when I felt the shift in our relationship; the emotional attachment seemed to fade. There had been many occasions when I had wanted to ask 'Everything' if and when he might be ready to marry me, but the fear of putting him off or losing him stopped me from doing so. There were times when we had invited some of our Christian friends over to fellowship with us, but when the dreaded subject area broached the topic of marriage there was an obvious shift in his body language which screamed, "No!" 'Everything' was not comfortable with discussing our future with others and became seemingly despondent in any conversations about our future. It was clear that marriage was not something he wanted to do, but he never seemed to ever verbalise it to confirm the fact. We both were silent, not admitting how we truly felt about each other when individually we knew what we both wanted and our desires came into conflict. I wanted the marriage whilst he did not and it seemed that nothing was going to change in order to move either of us forward, one way or another.

It was a New Year, and with the Year came some new resolutions. I desperately wanted to see a deeper commitment with 'Everything' but I knew that unless I asked him the direct question of, "Will you or won't you?" I would remain in limbo, not knowing where we were headed. I thought about consulting God through prayer, but at the same time I felt that I couldn't go to The Father for counsel. I had already fallen into the habit of sporadic prayer; in fact it was obvious I still had not recovered from the trauma of the failed baptism the month before, so I wasn't sure where I could turn. I had also made a mess of things by moving into the new home with 'Everything' where in only three short weeks of being together, we were already falling apart. The warning signs from God were seemingly coming to pass in quick succession, and I was amazed at what was unfolding before me. I went back and forth in my thoughts and emotions, debating if I had enough courage to ask him if he would ever want to marry me. I was terrified as to what the answer might have been, but I knew that we could not carry on in limbo and lacking direction. I knew that there was a 50/50 chance of the outcome not going in my favour, but it was a chance I was willing to take. A part of me was in denial, believing that our relationship would never come to an end and that we could survive any storm. I had seen others helped and encouraged through our relationship, but mostly I knew what it had done for me, and so I would cling on to that with hope. However, there was a huge part of me that knew intuitively the relationship was coming to an end and that the answer would be "no".

In the days leading up to the night of the 25th of January I went back and forth in my mind over the implications of asking 'Everything' when he might be willing to have me as his wife. It was a period of both excitement and preparation for bereavement. I spent most of the time reflecting back on our relationship, thinking about how far we had come and just how wonderful things were when we worked together as a team. I also thought about all the difficulties and how much we had both changed. We had both become creatures of habit and moving into the new place had neither grown us spiritual or brought us any closer together as I had hoped. All that our new situation did was act as a band aid, covering over the old wounds and keeping them from healing. I had wanted to see the love grow, but somehow it was stifled. Still I was determined to know for definite where his heart was and if he still wanted to marry me as he had said in the past or if he had changed his mind. Either way, a conclusion to the chapter on me and 'Everything' had to be realised.

The day of the 25th of January had been a relatively uneventful one, with the usual routine of work in the day and going to the gym in the evening. I had psyched myself up all day to speak with 'Everything', switching between being fired up and being scared to finally express the truth of what was in my heart.

There were no issues or conflict between us at the time and I was excited to get home, in from the cold, and to the man I still loved despite the difficulties. My heart was racing, but as usual he was calm and relaxed in his demeanour which in turn relaxed me. I had always loved coming home to 'Everything'. As I walked up the stairs to our home after each working day, I would look forward to seeing him and hearing his voice, and this night was no different. As I browed the top of our stairs, 'Everything' was in the kitchen washing the dishes. He asked me how my day had been and went on to explain that he was preparing dinner for us that night, as I kicked off my shoes and coat. Our home felt peaceful and as I sat back on the sofa, I began to feel synchronised with the peace surrounding me and a growing confidence filled me to the core. We continued on in general conversation and as we exchanged information, I began steering our conversation towards the subject matter of our relationship as soon as I felt comfortable and confident that I could, but things abruptly changed for the worse. Until that very moment, I had sat back comfortably and content as I allowed myself to become lost in my own imagination of being Mrs 'Everything'. His voice was music to my soul even in the hazy mist of a failing relationship, and as I listened to the softness of his voice I reminisced on a love that was once so true. In those short split seconds, it felt as though I were floating on a cloud and it didn't matter what was to come next, but as his voice became sterner and more severe, I was brought back from my fantasy to the harsh reality of the words "I do not want to get married".

Among the many thoughts that were engulfing my brain whilst 'Everything' paced back and forth to and from the fridge, my mind was cast back to the night of my failed baptism. That night in my sadness and exhaustion, I had heard a clear instruction from the Holy Spirit that I needed to place God first in all things, but primarily over 'Everything'. It was a test of my faithfulness being told to give him up and to heed instruction, but I couldn't do it. I knew that I had been asked to make a choice in order that God could move through my life and take control. God and God alone was to be the light in my darkness and to be my hero and strength, not 'Everything'. I finally accepted that there had been a very evident warning time and time again over my choices, and as I reflected even further on my decision to move into the new home with 'Everything, I knew that my decision to do so had set the ball in motion for God to have to take an active stand in disciplining me for my open disobedience. In that very moment I knew that it was over in our relationship, but I still fought against it in my heart as I looked at 'Everything' and listened to his explanation for why he did not want to get married. My sadness was all encompassing because not only had I failed at my relationship with 'Everything', I had also failed myself but mostly I had failed God. In the realisation of what was unfolding, I knew that I had to break up with 'Everything'. Our relationship was never going to be good anymore because God was no longer any real part of the crucial process. It could not bear good fruit because our foundations were not on good soil, but I still made a mistake in believing that

I could succeed by my own strength or even that of the strength of 'Everything' and mine combined. However, it was only through God that there could ever be any real victory in our relationship and although I understood it all too well, I couldn't accept my relationship was over, and so the pull of my flesh kept me looking for answers even when I should have stopped trying to do so and just listened to the direction of God. I struggled with knowing that there was no choice and that a sacrifice had to be made with immediate effect.

All I could see was the pain of our failed relationship nothing more or nothing less. It was all the more difficult because despite the break up between 'Everything' and I in the January, we still lived under the same roof until the August of that year. It was impossible to remain in any consistency and I spent the following seven months not knowing if I were coming or going emotionally. We literally went from separation to platonic friends, to a restoration of closeness without commitment, then reunited but then back to nothing more than two people living under the same roof. In a brief moment of kindness towards one another, there was a silver lining in a dark cloud where we were briefly reunited in our relationship together mid-summer, but something was still not right. Whilst we agreed to work on things in order to move forward together, something was missing in each of us and that thing was that we were still both spiritually discontent. I, in particular, felt close to spiritual emptiness. I knew that I had not fully reconciled the situation with God, placing Him at the centre of all things with trust and surrender, nor did I know how to because I was still madly and deeply in love with 'Everything' and I desperately wanted to succeed at our relationship. Despite officially being separated I missed him, and daily life just wasn't the same without him despite my relationship with God. However we continued to live together in a place of crisis and struggle, and as a result it was not long before we were back to not exercising any love or affection toward each other even as two people who had once been close. I found myself lonely again and would often go to bed in tears whilst I listened to 'Everything' through the wall next door. There were times where, in a desperate attempt to communicate with him without getting lost in an argumentative or a misunderstanding spirit, I would text 'Everything' to share with him just how much I missed him and that I was lonely without his real presence in my life. I felt limited in my resources and it was the only way then that I knew how to express myself without dispute. I wanted there to be a real change for 'Everything' with his love for me returning, but once again I could feel him slipping through my fingers even further away. I pondered over the thought that perhaps things were not right because I had still not grasped the reality of the shift in emotions which were seemingly becoming permanent, but again I ignored the obvious and pressed on with my own plans. I was determined to win back his love and I would not give up on him despite struggling and fighting against an inevitable end.

CHAPTER 11

Struggling

I had spent a number of days trying to work out what it was that I could do to try and inject some fun back into the seriousness of our failing relationship despite not officially being together as a couple. Both myself and 'Everything' had experienced a tough few months emotionally where we had each been dealing with other challenges outside of our home. It all seemed to be taking its toll but somehow, instead of turning to each other to be that help and support, we continued to keep our distance respectively. I could see that 'Everything' was tired of the constant struggle but I wasn't sure how to reach out to him. I had wanted to be that person for him again; the one who he talked to and trusted but instead I had become part of the biggest challenge in his life and I understood that I could no longer be that source of comfort and light anymore. I hated knowing that I was contributing to any of his suffering but I didn't know what to do and in not knowing what to do or what he truly needed, I often got it wrong whenever I would try to fix things. Sometimes 'Everything' seemed to just need some breathing space, but I always took it as rejection. Often I would respond in hostility and chastisement through sheer frustration, but then on reflection I would head off to a quiet space on my own and cry in frustration over my handling of things. I didn't know how to really express myself without telling him off and I felt awful because of it. I would often come away from our conversations full of regret about how I managed them, but again I was not turning to God for counsel. I still could not quite correlate allowing God to lead in healing and resolving the relationship conflict as being the answer. I still felt the need to lead and repair what only God could do but I no longer held any of the tools nor would I have known what to do with them had they been firmly placed in my grip. The skillset belonged to The Father, but my trust in Him was still questionable. Once again I allowed myself to get lost in the lesson. I was too impatient to wait on God and I most certainly did not want to hand 'Everything' over to Him as the rightful treasurer of his heart. However, it was not just about 'Everything'....what about my own heart? I had forgotten that it was also about handing myself over to God. The journey was not solely about 'Everything'. God loved us both equally and He had wanted to rescue us both but still I struggled with surrendering to His will for my life. Instead of releasing my pain and suffering to Him I guarded my heart even more ignoring

the promptings of the Holy Spirit. I had known for the longest time
that The Holy Spirit was still there trying desperately to bring me
round to the will of The Father, but I didn't know how to let Him
in. I was afraid. I was still afraid that if I were to let go, 'Everything'
would be gone forever and I couldn't take that risk. I wouldn't and
so I gathered what strength I had left and decided that I would give
my all to 'Everything' in whatever capacity he needed. I was going
to do whatever it took to be the stable and reliable woman in his life
again, and I was going to do it with purpose and conviction.

The morning of the 18th July I woke up with a determined
attitude and felt fired up in my spirit, claiming that it was going to
be the day to change things around for the better. I was tired and
worn down by the continuous struggle and miscommunication
between 'Everything' and I over the six month period of
uncertainty and confusion and simply wanted the two of us to just
start enjoying each other's company again. It seemed as if our day to
day interactions were always met with some debate over where we
were in our relationship, what we should be doing and what each of
us were doing wrong. From my perspective, up until that moment,
I struggled to hear or accept anything as a positive whenever
'Everything' would suggest what we needed to do in order to help
move things forward. I had become overly sensitive and continued
on in feeling suspicious of his motives, growing in ignorance to
hearing anything which might have helped. I had become tone
deaf and to make matters worse there was no real consulting of

God through prayer in the very many decisions I made concerning 'Everything'.

The beginning of the day of July 18th had been no exception. I had made a decision to plan what I felt was to be an amazing day of fun spent with 'Everything', but to do so without even so much as a whisper to God asking for guidance over the day was a recipe for disaster. In my heart of hearts I knew it was wrong and I felt a kind of conviction similar to when we were planning our move to the new home. I was now mature enough in my walk with God to know better but still exercised my dependence on spiritual milk through acting as if I was strong enough to lead the way through to victory, solely by my own efforts. No man (or woman) of God has the capacity to walk their path without falling among thorns if they try to do so independently of God and at this point I was being choked by them as I tried to fight my way out of them. Still I pressed on with my plans for taking 'Everything' out on a surprise trip, hoping he would be excited not just about the day but also in spending some quality time with me. We had not been out together socially in a long time so I was eager in my anticipation as to what lay ahead. The day's activities were not anything overly inventive, just a trip to the local golfing range to have a bit of let loose fun - something we desperately needed. I tried my hardest to forget our problems for just a moment and be a fun loving "girlfriend" rather than the insecure "nag" I had started to become. I batted away any feelings of insecurities as I noticed that my efforts to have fun with 'Everything' were proving futile.

He seemed distant and indifferent towards me and it felt as if he really did not want to be there. Still, I carried on ignoring his lack of presence by laughing and joking around, trying to make the day as fun as possible by creating new memories, but it didn't seem to work and just as my golfing targets seemed impossible with each swing, so was my attempt to break back through into 'Everything's' heart.

However, I wasn't ready to quit or throw in the towel just yet. There was just too much at stake. I truly believed that if I could just reach him with a reminder of who I once was to him, then I would be able to start melting away the solid encasement of his emotions but I didn't feel confident enough to succeed. In a moment of desperation, I reached for a past memory of a time we had been close to help me in my declining confidence. I reflected on a day when we lay on my couch silently listening to worship music; I had just moved into a new place and had nothing but the sofa. I could remember lying there, not understanding much of anything about his heart or God's heart, but knowing there was a peace and a joy that surpassed my knowledge. It was 'Everything' that had first shown me an example of Christ's love for me and in that moment of reflection, I suddenly felt lifted in my spirit, enough so to replace my failing energy. I looked back at 'Everything' with a smile and reached for his hand, but as our hands connected to join as one, he stiffened up. I looked at him for confirmation of his actions as to be sure I had interpreted it right, but instead he avoided eye contact with me. 'Everything' was just not there, neither did he want to be.

By the time we sat down to eat at a local restaurant later that evening, it was becoming increasingly obvious that the day was not working out as I had planned and by this stage 'Everything' seemed irritated by every word or action I took. He was snappy and agitated, but mostly he seemed angry. In an attempt to have a moment to gather my panicked thoughts I decided to make a quick exit to try and gain some control over the failing situation, so I excused myself from the table giving the excuse that I needed to go to the local shop for a moment and I quickly left the restaurant. As I walked slowly and thought deeply, I acknowledged that the day had been unsuccessful and I felt as though I had failed. I was scared, and in that moment I turned to God asking for His mercy and help but mostly for the strength to hear what 'Everything' might have had to say. I waited until I felt a sense of calm and once it was received I walked back into the restaurant, sat down at the table and in a softly spoken voice asked him what was wrong. As I waited for his response, he held his head down in his hands, scratched his hair and uttered the words that he was struggling with our relationship. Then there was silence.

I sat back and took a deep breath in. I felt somewhat light headed and faint from what I could only describe as a direct result of the shock on hearing those very words "I am struggling." Whilst we sat there quietly – both searching for the right things to say to each other, our food was served but I couldn't eat. I couldn't even focus on what was on the plate as my eyes were welling up with tears, and the strain of holding them back sent pain searing through my throat. I needed to get out of there, I needed to escape the increasingly pressurised environment so we had our food bagged up and began the long walk home. It felt as if we were walking for hours and with each step, my body felt heavier as if my soul was being weighed down by an unseen force. I wanted to hurry in the direction of home so that I could release all of the built up tears behind closed doors, but I also did not want to go home to face the very thing I had been avoiding for the past few months. I was scared and I didn't want to hear anymore. I didn't feel able to cope with the utter devastation that was overtaking my whole being in that very moment, but I needed to listen and allow 'Everything' to be heard. Once we got home, he continued on to explain how he was feeling and I had no choice but to listen and accept his truth. For once, I owed it to him to listen and not brush off or over his feelings placing mine first as I had done in the past. Although I had already guessed how he had felt I had never really heard it, and to hear him speak about being unsure and apprehensive in the physical was like taking a bullet. This was a man who in the past didn't care what we did or where we were as long as he was with me, but in the present he was expressing that he was unsure if he even still felt any love towards me. Despite my obvious distress at the unfolding news, I couldn't let us remain in the limbo of uncertainty and I had to take action. After digesting the shock of hearing 'Everything' confess his struggles with our relationship, I felt moved to take action. Although I was uncertain of what to do, I knew that something had to be done. It was hard to hear the truth especially as I already knew it but had fallen into the trap of thinking I could ignore the warning signs, particularly when they had already come from God. The truth of his words had such an impact on me, whereby I was left feeling confused and not knowing what to do for the best, but again I didn't consult God. I didn't listen for His voice nor did I ask for His help when I so desperately needed it and so my initial response was to pack up some clothes and go to stay with a friend for a while.

I concluded that I needed to take myself away from 'Everything' and out of the situation. I had finally taken the action I should had done months earlier when God has sent His Holy Spirit to encourage me to separate with 'Everything' in the beginning. The problem was that my actions came in the moment of crisis once 'Everything' confessed his struggles as opposed to acting on God's instruction. Once again I had decided on what I thought was best and not because I was being led to a spiritual conclusion. It was because I was losing my relationship. It was evidently coming to the end of its cycle and so I decided that the only way to deal with it effectively was to run and that is what I did. If I am honest with myself, I thought that perhaps if I took myself away from the situation and out of the equation by leaving our home and showing 'Everything' I was serious enough to take action, it would force him to think about what he might be losing. However, my leaving did not seem to change his viewpoint. Whilst I knew when I decided to leave 'Everything' would not fall to his knees in tears begging me to stay, I was sure that my leaving would cause some kind of reaction. Little did I know my leaving would not create the desired effect. I thought that 'Everything' would begin to crumble and that he would realise me not being there created a void in his life. I thought that he would miss me, but I came to see that my leaving had the exact opposite effect. The first night away from 'Everything' I went to stay with our close friend Sonia. As I arrived at her home I sat on her floor stunned at the outcome of events as I recounted what had happened in order to make sense of it. Subsequent weeks away from 'Everything' saw my emotions rise and fall quicker than a rollercoaster and I spent evenings crying inconsolably into the arms of loved ones who did their best to comfort me. In 'Everything' I did not see the reaction of a man broken or that of a man who had lost something or someone meaningful and valuable to him. Whenever I would take trips back to our home to collect some clothing, 'Everything' seemed for the most part relaxed. Whilst there seemed to be a glint of sadness in his eyes, he remained silent. His lack of response and minimal contact during my time away from our home confused me greatly. I remained in a state of mourning while he seemingly embraced the change with a moment of clarity.

I found it hard being away from 'Everything' and consulted the many irrational thoughts that can attack your mind when you try to work things out on your own. I missed him terribly, but instead of using the time away to focus on myself and build a better relationship with God, I continued to focus on 'Everything'. I still hadn't fully accepted the spiritual lesson and holding onto him was all that I knew how to do. Keeping 'Everything' in focus was all that made me feel sane and whole, and the only thing that made sense in my life. I knew in my rational thinking that I was not adopting the right attitude by making 'Everything' my all but I did not care; I just wanted to be right with him again. To me, 'Everything' was real and tangible in the ever present, whereas God was reality of a next life. I never questioned who God was and I wanted to be a faithful servant but my attention was not solely on Him. I truly believed that, despite my lack of focus, God would forgive me for putting 'Everything' first because He knew and truly understood what my intentions were despite the misguidance. However, I knew deep down it was wrong to think and act that way, and could only lead to my spiritual destruction as well as destroy my relationship with 'Everything' for good. It is very true and some might say a sobering reality that when you question God, ignore His instruction or choose not to place Him at the centre of your life before all things, then you can be likely to fail in all that you do especially if you have truly known God and this was happening to me.

At the time I was desensitised to the reality that I was creating my very own self-fulfilling prophecy which was forcing a complete breakdown, but I was going to press on with focusing on him, the man that was 'Everything'. I wanted to find a way to have his acceptance and love back and so I went again to work on my own individual plans. I came up with an idea, deciding to put on a surprise birthday party for him with the help of Sonia who was supporting me through the emotional turbulence. As it was a milestone birthday I wanted him to feel special because to me, he was still so special and I felt that he deserved all adoration. I did not want to let the current status of our relationship deter my plans or ruin what I wanted for him, so I carried on with organising it. I knew that 'Everything' had struggled, in part, with believing that he was cared for and loved; not so much by me as it was obvious how much I loved him at the time, but perhaps my love had just became a commonplace love to him and one that no longer carried any weight. Nevertheless, I knew that it was important for 'Everything' to feel the love and support of his family and friends and I wanted him to have that. So in spite of the struggles he was facing with me moving out and with us living very separate lives, I pressed on with planning his party. The night was a memorable one, if only just for seeing that brief moment of real happiness on his face as he walked in to hugs and kisses from all those who made an effort to support him with love by their attendance. Friends from church, friends from his past, family and clients were all there to wish him well and being greeted with such acknowledgement did something amazing for 'Everything' which I think even he did not expect. I believe it made something cross over in him. I believe it made 'Everything' feel truly loved and appreciated in perhaps a way he had not previously known during the time of our relationship. I saw a difference in his face and a change in his demeanour. He was happy.

It was as if the party gave 'Everything' the confidence to know that it wasn't just me anymore. It wasn't just me that was there to love him...a love that he was used to and a love that he had probably grown tired of. It seemed as if he had a renewed sense of self, a renewed sense of self believe and increased self-worth.

One afternoon, in the final days of our relationship, 'Everything' and I had a conversation about the party; he seemed very reflective. He thanked me for organising such a good night and again confirmed how much he had enjoyed it. As I listened closely to the hopefulness of his voice, I then heard him say something of significance. He went on to explain that he felt differently and when I asked him how, he said that he could not explain it other than he felt as if he was worth something. I can remember an all too familiar sense of fear and panic overwhelm me as he said, "I feel like I am worth something." It began setting off major alarm bells in my mind and hearing those very words told me something. Those very words placed firmly on my heart telling me that 'Everything' no longer needed me anymore. I spent the rest of my day playing the words over and over in my mind. I couldn't seem to shake them off and again I felt exhausted by the continuous audit trail of unhappiness that seemed to always be associated with 'Everything'. I knew it wasn't his fault nor was it mine, but in my mind I wondered when the difficulty was ever going to end. I was still living with Sonia away from our home and desperately wanted to move back in with 'Everything' but I felt afraid to ask and after hearing his words, I felt like I couldn't. I didn't think he wanted me back, in fact I knew that he didn't and as I continued to play the words over in my mind, I felt fuelled with rejection and then the anger took over. I wanted answers. Real concrete answers from 'Everything' once and for all and I was not going to take no for an answer.

That evening I went back to our place and when 'Everything' came home our conversation transcended into an argument when I had confirmation that he was still struggling with his feelings towards me and that he was still unsure of our future. Even after a period of seemingly getting closer again and back on track, he still felt as though we both wanted different things. I didn't understand what he meant and in my lack of understanding felt confused, hurt and angry. I wanted him to explain himself and I can remember being sat on the floor waiting with baited breath as he sat down to join me on the floor at the opposite end of the lounge. He continued on saying very calmly that he could no longer do it anymore and I can remember in a moment of ignorance asking him very abruptly, "do what?" and as he stumbled on his words, he then followed up with, "I cannot do it any longer, it's over".

Even then I don't think I truly believed it or accepted that our relationship was over because in my mind we had been through too much together for it to be finished in what felt like a blink of an eye. Yes we had struggled, but until that point we had never been seemingly broken beyond repair. In an effort to hide behind my despair, I began immediately talking about separating the things we had bought and built up together over the years of our relationship. My tone became very matter of fact in an attempt to mask over how I was truly feeling – shocked and in disbelief. I couldn't believe it was over and thought that perhaps it was a phase, but it was finished once and for all. Our relationship had died and was now being finally laid to rest. The love of my life who had promised to love me - who had promised it was always me - no longer wanted to be with me had given up on me and thrown in the towel. He had given up when it got hard, given up when it was no longer fun for him, or perhaps he had given up because he had found something or someone else better. Despite the possible direction, I couldn't comprehend it and it left me feeling devastated. I can remember a few days later he moved out of our home and I returned to a place of emptiness. I can remember opening the front door and apprehensively walking up the stairs bracing myself for going into the unknown. At first, I turned and looked towards the bathroom and his toothbrush was gone and although it was only a small part of the many things he would have taken with him when he left, for me, it symbolised a significant part of 'Everything' that was removed from our home. He was truly gone. I looked around the rest of our place and it was spotless; the whole apartment had been cleaned from top to bottom. It was the kind of cleaning you do when you're coming to the end of a contract and you're leaving a place for good and that's exactly how our home looked. There was no trace of 'Everything' anywhere. The life I had known with him was gone. He was no longer present and then it hit me. My 'Everything' had gone and the feeling was unbearable. In my angst I dropped down to my knees before God amidst the emptiness and pleaded with Him to bring back my 'Everything'. I cried out to God asking why, asking what I had done that was so wrong to deserve 'Everything' being, what felt like, ripped away from my heart and soul. I begged and pleaded with God for forgiveness, but then felt angry towards God for punishing me by taking my love and placing me in abandonment. I was filled with conflict.

Suddenly, I felt a change in the atmosphere and I wasn't alone. Fear took over me as I felt a dark shadow around me. My whole body felt weak and as my spiritual guard broke down, I sensed the presence of the enemy. I was broken and fragmented, presenting the perfect opportunity to strike during my low point and that he did. I could hear his voice inside my mind telling me that 'Everything' never loved me and that he had lied from the very beginning of our relationship. As I tried to fight off his voice it became louder, telling me that I was not good enough and not pretty enough. I went and looked at myself in the mirror; my hair was a mess and my face now swollen and puffy from crying. As I looked at my reflection, I heard the voice say to me that he left because of my fake hair, ugly face and stretch marks. I closed my eyes and walked away from the mirror trying to ignore the lies which were starting to feel as though they were truth, but the voice would not leave me alone. The enemy went on to say that 'Everything' had left me because I was overbearing, a nag and a bore, and that it was because of my harshness, my age, my past but mostly because I was not "The One".

The enemy kept on and on at me until I fell into absolute despair and started believing his lies as truth. 'Everything' had gone and there was nothing left other than the sound of my tears and no-one to comfort me. I lay down on the floor huddled in the foetal position as the enemy continued to rock my spiritual cradle until I fell asleep broken and alone.

CHAPTER 12

Alone

Following the initial days after the 29th of August when 'Everything' had made the choice to end our relationship and leave, I experienced the darkest time of my life. I had experienced pain in the past before 'Everything' had come into my world, but nothing could compare to the utter devastation of losing the most important person in my life. I was broken into what felt like a million pieces. I couldn't see past anything, I couldn't hear anything and I couldn't feel anything other than the pain of him not being there and in my world anymore. I would wake each morning and for a split second have a moment of peace before his departure was realised, and I would go to bed each night with an unrealistic hope of him knocking on the front door and returning home. It was hard to deal with 'Everything' not being the first person I saw in the morning and the last thing at night. It was like taking a bullet each time piercing my heart. As I looked around our home not a trace of him was there. Constantly, I was reminded of the harsh reality of being alone and there was no way to escape it. At night I would try to ignore it by staying up late watching mostly fantasy adventure genre movies to escape my reality, but once the film was over I was back to not knowing what to do with myself. I would toss back and forth in bed with thoughts of 'Everything' and imagine him out partying, having the time of his life while I lay there inconsolable. I would try to ignore the harassing thoughts, but they kept 'Everything' active in my mind. I missed him terribly and often in a moment of weakness, I would reach for my phone to call him but could never bring myself to dial for fear of the response if he were to hear my voice at the other end, and so I would leave it.

Not hearing his voice each day was a deafening silence. I felt as if I no longer had a purpose; no longer did I have someone to cook for, to clean for, to look after and love. No longer was I able to focus all my attention towards my 'Everything' which took me away from focusing on myself and the trials of my own life, and it was back to being just me again. I was all that was left, so I had to deal with it but I did not want to. I felt as if something inside me had died. All the promises and all the things that I believed were going to happen – the future with my love, marriage, children, and my very own family...gone. All of my dreams were crushed and the pain was unbearable. The sadness was overwhelming and all I could think about was my love and the fact that he was gone, and it was impossible to believe. I knew that the road ahead wasn't going to be easy having to adjust back to single life but, in that moment, I couldn't even conceive of the possibility of surviving simply another day let alone any sort of future without 'Everything'. Just the thought of another week, a month or a year without him sent pain piercing through my heart and mind and I would cry uncontrollably whenever the reality of what I had to face would come over me. In a moment of anger I felt lied to by him and, to some extent, by God. It was a daily battle and one that saw me begin to care very little for myself as my thoughts began to descend further into a state of hopelessness. I couldn't seem to get past the point of wanting to get out of bed each day, nor did I want to eat much and was surviving on very little sleep. Life seemed to have little to no purpose and one that afforded me no answers as to when the pain would finally be over, and so I continued on in what felt like real suffering. Nothing could transcend my understanding of where I was in that very moment – in a state of despair. I was inconsolable and beyond reasoning. There were times when my sister Faith would come and sit with me in the evenings and watch on hopelessly as I lay on my sofa in tears, unable to take an ounce of comfort from her words or presence. There were times when a close friend Maria who had visited would refuse to leave until I had at least sipped on some tea, because she worried about my lack of eating. There were times when my best friend Amiyah, who was pregnant during the breakup, would travel from far on the bus just to sit with and hold me and although I felt supported and cared for by my loved ones, I couldn't get past the emptiness brought on by missing 'Everything'.

I didn't want to be alone because I feared my thoughts whenever I was, but at the same time I did not want to be in much company, and so I would hide away behind closed doors and sink further into a state of incapacitation. I would just lie there looking up into the atmosphere as my hope for release would perish. I would cry out to God through some sort of prayer asking for his release…begging for it, only to feel as if I had not been heard. I questioned God as to why I could feel the attack of the enemy so strongly but not the rescue of His Love. I would plead for God's forgiveness as I began to believe I was being punished for mistakes during my relationship with 'Everything' but it seemed as if I had been forsaken, as the enemy's presence continued to grow in momentum. I began to have thoughts of wanting to die. Not suicidal thoughts, but feeling that it was all too hard and painful to want to continue. I prayed to God for release; any kind of release that saw freedom from my suffering and so I asked The Father to take me as I felt ready to go home to Heaven. I no longer wanted to live a life without purpose or one that was riddled in guilt and shame. I couldn't see a future and was filled with fear of the unknown. I looked at my life and could no longer see what I had to offer in the world. I was of an age which I believed forged a difficult place for starting again and I felt as if I were damaged beyond repair. In my mind, I had nothing left to give. I was tired and beaten, and just wanted it all to stop. However, there was something in me that knew that asking God to take me home was not going to happen and so my prayers began to change. I first asked God to simply help me. I didn't have many words, but just enough to call upon Him and to draw on His strength somehow. As I felt a grain of peace come over me; I grew a little more in faith which further helped me to ask The Father for courage and strength to face the day ahead. I knew that I couldn't do too much too soon, and so I focused only on being able to cope in that present moment with God's help. At first it felt like a conscious effort to pray in faith for strength especially as I didn't feel like it, but I began to notice that I was getting through each day that bit easier. I was surviving. God's strength was helping me although I still felt like I was only making it by the skin of my teeth. I was still emotional and felt a sense of loneliness, but I also sensed a presence of the Holy Spirit despite the fogginess of my feelings.

As the weeks steadily began to go by, again my prayers began to change. I would ask God to give me the strength to remain and endure. I did not like how I felt or what I was going through, but I felt a real sense of needing to be in a place where God could really reach down inside me. I was broken, but as I began to accept my brokenness before The Father, I noticed that the guilt and shame began to shift and with it came an acceptance of the process. I knew that God wanted to work with me to heal me, but it was not going to be easy because I still had so much attachment to 'Everything' and so my prayers began to change again. I asked

God to give me the strength to let 'Everything' go but first I had to work within myself to truly believe in what I was asking for. A part of me had no real desire to do so, but I knew that I had to begin to at least ask the right things through prayer so that God's perfect love could heal my broken heart. It was a back and forward battle in my attempt to draw closer to Him, as I tried effortlessly to focus on Jesus and what He was doing for me as to opposed to the lies of the enemy and what I felt I had lost. I tried to remain in the present and with the Holy Spirit rather than look back trying to find answers in what was dead, but my mind still struggled as I felt it firmly stuck in my emotions. I continued to ask God for answers as I went from feeling perfectly okay in one moment and then back to despair in another, but through it all I tried desperately to fix my mind on Jesus and just hold on. I knew that if there was nothing else I could do, I needed to cling to God's hope and for the very first time in my life I called on God and tried earnestly to surrender to His will.

At first it felt alien to me to try and give it all over to God, but I would continually pray to Him for re-assurance which was comforting and would calm me whenever I felt as if I were losing control. There were times when again I did not want to lean on God and I was distracted with negative thoughts from the enemy. There were times when the all too familiar sense of hopelessness returned and it felt too difficult to keep pressing on for a breakthrough. When it felt pointless, when it felt too painful and when there were times I just did not believe that God would pull me through, I wanted to give up. It was not because

I thought The Father was incapable of rescuing me, but it was because I thought that I was undeserving of any rescue. I felt that perhaps my suffering was to teach me a lesson which I had not yet learnt, especially as my thinking strayed back and forth in trusting that God loved me completely and would do as He had always promised. I continued to try and fight against the battle in my mind that kept me straying away from God, back to accepting that only Jesus could direct my sinking ship through the storm to safety. I tried my best to focus more on prayer and letting go of what was old and allowing Jesus to give me that which was greater, and that is what I did – little by little. I continued on with small breathy prayers in meditation of becoming stronger, as I tried my best to focus and seek comfort in confiding in The Lord. I listened to worship music with certain songs on repeat to feel lifted in my spirit. I read the Word of God, seeking out scriptures that spoke directly to my need and the situation I faced, and I would take comfort from those who prayed for and supported me. I soon came to the realisation that I couldn't do it alone and needed pastoral care, so I began to meet regularly with my church leader, Pastor John. Initially our meetings were very difficult for me as we discussed the history of my relationship with 'Everything', leaving my last church and the breakdown of our relationship. I often sat in tears with a lack of any real understanding and a hope for answers that would just make me feel better, but mostly I felt a sense of release and a hope for the future as I was encouraged to seek God and remain in faith. It helped me greatly as I had always felt a sense of judgement for my previous choices, but in counsel with Pastor John I felt a sense of understanding and acceptance of who I was despite my failings. It gave me motivation, even though I was far from any real victory, but I finally felt as if there was someone on my side and a person who was really interceding on my behalf and standing in the gap for my recovery.

Things started to feel as though they were really moving forward, but then the feeling of loneliness would creep back over me as I was reminded of the void 'Everything' had left in my life. I missed his presence. I tried to fight against it, but there was always something to remind me that I was alone and that he was never coming home. Not only that, but as the days and weeks kept rolling by, it was a reminder that it was another day or week that I had not seen 'Everything' creating more distance which would fade our chapter to just a memory. I did not know where he was or what he was doing and it was hard not knowing if he was okay. As I sat most evenings in contemplation about what might be going on in his life, I felt tempted by the enemy to do things that were not for my greater good. In desperation of not knowing and by a means to somehow be in some sort of contact with 'Everything' I began checking on him via social media. It was never to check up on him as such, but only as a way for me to see him and stay close to him albeit in the virtual realm. It never made any sense to me to take an action that would ultimately cause me pain, but I felt I had no other way to reach him and so I would look at pictures and status updates as a means of having some sort of contact. It made me happy to see he was happy, but things quickly began to change when I saw something that suggested he had moved on and was possibly happy with someone else. Again I felt broken, but instead of walking away from my actions, I felt tempted to delve deeper into finding out more. A part of me did it in the hope that I would not find anything at all, but eventually I found something that confirmed there was someone else and no going back for us as a couple.

Nothing could prepare me for the returning pain and agony I felt at the confirmation that our relationship and his love for me was well and truly over. The sight of seeing 'Everything' in a picture in the arms of another woman nearly destroyed me. In that very moment I dropped down in the middle of the street, as the pure anguish took over my whole body. My legs literally gave way from underneath me as I sat down in a heap, doubled over in my grief as Sonia and another friend tried to lift me up and comfort me. I couldn't breathe or even mutter any words that made audible sense in the distress of what I had seen, but it was my own fault. Had I not been looking and seeking out information I would never have found out or seen the images of them happy, but I couldn't help but fixate on it. Again I felt as I were ready for The Lord to take me and in a moment of asking for that release I felt a battle within as my thoughts and feelings were pulled between the light and darkness. Close friends and family rallied around me in support as I continued to sink further into a place of bereavement, but something was not letting me go and I know that it was God, and although in that moment I could not bring myself to lift my voice in prayer, I knew that The Father was sticking close by me. The following days saw much difficulty and the support of those closest to me was all that got me through as friends sat next to me and literally watched me until I would fall asleep often into my tears. It was difficult for all that were close to me, but I felt grateful to have such a solid support network when I didn't have very much to give others at the time. As I reflected on those who may have gone through similar situations to me or worse, those who did not have such good friends as I did, I began to feel even more blessed that God had sent His angels to watch over me. Although in pain, I still felt a sense of hope in the human kindness of all that selflessly supported my struggles. I realised that I wasn't alone anymore and despite the nightmare I was facing, I would get through it with the help of those that showed me continued love and kindness.

Going back to church after the incident was hard as I sat amongst the congregation in inconsolable tears, but being in my spiritual home was the only place where the peace of God would wash over me. It cleansed me – even if it felt just for a moment, and was what I needed. Church leadership continued to pray for my deliverance, trying to break any connections or soul ties that I carried with 'Everything' in an attempt to start breaking down any spiritual strongholds. Initially I did not understand the need to be separated from 'Everything' in this way and a part of me wanted to continue in having that link to him as I still struggled to let him go, but every time I met with Pastor John for a time of pastoral care,

I got a bit stronger in letting go and moving forward. I felt lighter, as if something was being stretched and lifted out of me but I was faced with an upheaval when out of the blue, 'Everything' returned to our home to collect some of his belongings. I can remember being defensive and cold towards him as if he was a stranger, but it was the only way I knew how to protect myself. In truth I felt further from the façade I was presenting towards him and as I turned away to walk into another room whilst he collected what was needed, I squeezed my eyes tightly in a way to stop myself and regain focus from wanting to run into his arms begging him to stay. After he left, I prayed and questioned God over the continual disruption to my feelings with some kind of episode or another. It seemed that whenever I would make a little bit of headway, something would happen to put me right back to square one and it was exhausting. Not only that, but whenever 'Everything' and I had some contact which was mostly centred around the apartment which he still paid towards, it always ended badly. I often felt sucked back into raking up the past or blaming him for something whilst he accused me of not changing, so in an attempt to stop the hurt that our contact brought for both of us, I blocked any contact from him by barring any calls and texts from his phone to mine. I didn't want to do it, but I felt as if I had no choice. I needed to try and move on even if it were only through pigeon steps; I needed to keep it moving forward.

Eventually I began to feel better and my time with God in prayer developed. Each day my voice got louder and stronger as I began declaring biblical truth in what God said about who I was in Christ and what I meant to Him. I began focusing on His plans for my prosperity, peace and joy that came by the grace of our Lord Jesus Christ. I began focusing on the truth that His strength was made perfect in my weakness as I started to let go of the things I could not control and as I focused more on God I began to let 'Everything' go just that little bit more. I still missed him and longed for answers and in an attempt to try and understand, I returned to my old church to speak with the church leadership there. I didn't know what I wanted to say or why I even travelled back there but I felt led to do so. I was nervous, as it meant going back to face a part of my past that I had not dealt with. It meant facing my fears over judgement, but I was reminded by the Holy Spirit not to pick back up that guilt or shame, as Christ had set me free from it. So I walked back into my old place of worship and sat down with Pastor Geoff. As I choked back tears trying to explain clearly what had happened, he reassured me that the church had always tried to support both 'Everything' and I and he knew of the difficulties we faced. I looked at him with a questioning look of expression on my face, because I had convinced myself that Pastor Geoff and other church leadership had always seen me as the problem. I believed that the church had seen me as the woman who had corrupted 'Everything' in his walk with God, when it was the complete opposite. Pastor Geoff went on to say that he could see I was making progress in my walk with God and then he apologised for what had happened with my failed baptism and as I sat listening to him I realised something. I had gone to the church in search of answers concerning my failed relationship with 'Everything' but instead I got answers concerning my own unresolved issues with the church. I realised that being led back to my old place of worship was purely for me and had nothing to do with 'Everything'. It was for me to gain peace over my relationship with the church and all that had happened there. As I continued listening to Pastor Geoff, I felt a release and then he said something of significance. He wanted to invite me back to the church, not only to return as part of its membership, but to have my baptism. I felt overwhelmed with happiness; a feeling I had not felt for some time. I sat there with what had changed from tears of despair to a sense of joy in anticipation of a future and a new one in Christ.

I returned home pondering over what had taken place. It had been a difficult part of my life dealing with not being baptised because I had wanted to give my life to Christ openly for so long. I had wanted to belong to Him and not only that, I wanted to move onto the next level with Him. I knew that I had lots of work to do, but felt confident I could do anything with Christ by my side. I felt excited but then I felt conflicted. Was I actually ready to be baptised? Not only that, how could I be baptised at a place I no longer worshipped at? As much as I desired to take that step forward as offered, I was in another place of worship at the Fellowship Church which was the place for my pastoral care. Despite being relatively new to the church I was attending, I felt settled and on my way. I wanted to continue being a part of the fellowship I had with my current church but I desired to have Jesus in my life on a deeper level and so I turned to God in prayer. I asked Him to give me clarity on what to do, and exercising the patience I had always struggled with, I waited on Him to give me a sign. I continued on in attending the Fellowship Church and having regular meetings with Pastor John to work through my struggles. I continued to think over and pray about whether or not it was time for me to be baptised and if I were truly ready, but God did not leave me too long without answers and I got what I knew was clarity from The Father. I was also offered to be baptised at the Fellowship Church, my new spiritual home.

I suddenly realised something of great significance; that God had heard me and did in fact answer prayers and not only that - my prayers. He had listened to the desires of my heart and responded clearly in the appointed time. He had waited until He knew I was ready and called me by name. I felt overwhelmed as a rush of warmth came over me. I realised in that very moment that I was going to survive being without 'Everything' and that it would all be alright, and that I would be just fine. I realised that as I began to work on and through the hindrances, the blessings were beginning to come forth. As I thought deeper into it, a moment of clarity revealed that as I began to trust God to take control of my life and I started to release 'Everything' over to His care, I simultaneously was allowing God into my heart first hand and slowly He was moving me forward. I praised God in that moment for what felt like undeserved favour and I gave thanks for His magnificent holiness.

I was not alone, nor would I ever be ever again.

CHAPTER 13

Baptism

From the moment it became clear that finally it was my time
to move forward and be baptised, I knew that I wanted to do it
at the Fellowship Church. Despite kindly being invited to have
the ceremony at my old place of worship and a place where my
spiritual journey had begun, it was my new church and current
spiritual home where I wanted to openly give my life to Christ.
The Fellowship Church was the place where God had started to
reach me on a more intimate level and it was where my growth and
maturity had flourished. In the past, my place of worship was not
one where God was able to do very much with me simply because
my motives for being there were that of a compromise. Yes, I had
wanted to grow in my Christian walk, but I desired more of an
approval from 'Everything' rather than that of The Father. For
that reason I felt I could never have remained there at the time,

especially during the breakup. I knew that I needed to be away from it all and in a place obscure from the public eye where only God could see me and heal me from the inside out. I needed to be truly alone with God but in the beginning it was not easy and a reality which I struggled with because I fought against what was needed. In my lack of understanding, I battled with wanting to work through my spiritual struggles because it had felt so difficult as I also struggled to make sense of God's logic throughout the latter part of my relationship with 'Everything' until its end. Nonetheless God so desired and loved me and was determined not to let me go, so it was in the Fellowship Church where eventually I got my will back to start again and grow in the acceptance of the stretching and moulding that was to shape my very being.

I had been a member of the Fellowship Church for the best part of a year and during the varying stages of my breakup with 'Everything'. I had first been introduced to the church as a visitor during a more positive time in our relationship, when a mutual friend invited both 'Everything' and I to attend a service. During our first visit to the Fellowship Church it didn't leave a lasting impression on me, as I compared it to my then regular place of worship. At the time it seemed all too small and inferior in comparison with the grander scale church I was attending, but the new Fellowship Church was to be the very place to pick up the pieces of my fragmented faith and devastated emotions when 'Everything' left me . It was a small building, placed halfway down and towards the end of a quiet road with an intimate congregation of welcoming faces. At first my interest in attending was of convenience and one of a means to an end in order that I could gain spiritual fuelling of some sort. I lacked any real commitment to the church, in fact, any one place of worship as I was not sure if I wanted to be a part of any congregation of believers. I had first begun attending a few months after leaving my last church prior to the end of my relationship with 'Everything', at a time when I questioned my faith and was not even sure I still felt any connection to my Christian walk. For me, it was a place to attend but not to grow. At the end of each service, sneakily I would leave in a quick attempt to avoid being noticed or to engage in any real sense of fellowship. In the beginning, I had no real interest in meeting with Pastor John or any senior members due to my very evident lack of trust in spiritual leadership, nor did I have a desire to get to know and meet God's people who formed part of the church's structure at the time. I just wanted to get in and out; to be able to reconcile within myself that I had fulfilled my weekly Christian duty by attending church on a Sunday. Sadly, I had made no connection with it. I placed a blockade around myself for protection and in it, felt a sense of security as I more or less isolated myself from anyone being able to help facilitate a reconnection to and an acceptance of God during a time of great stretching and discipline.

After 'Everything' left I continued on in a sense of spiritual stagnation, but I knew things had to change. I was not moving forward and whilst I was not in the greatest place emotionally and was struggling to cope with very much, I knew that how I felt would continue to supress me. I didn't like being what I knew to be a Sunday Christian as it left me feeling unfulfilled. I was already struggling with the void caused by the absence of 'Everything' and could feel myself descending further into spiritual chaos. I decided that I had to regain some control despite not feeling motivated to do so, but I knew that I would not succeed by my own strength. I needed help and knew that the only way to get the intervention I needed, was to go back to the Fellowship Church and fully integrate myself with the congregation and that is what I did but I hated it. At first I felt like a lost stranger amongst the crowd. I felt as if people were watching me as I often sat in tears during worship, but things steadily became easier as I began to get to know people and make friends. The fellowship was kind and nurturing towards me and I always felt safe there. I felt strangely at ease with being what I felt was stripped bare and naked for all to see, because I knew that I was truly with God's people who cared and wanted to see me get through my emotional difficulties and spiritual battles to a real place of victory. No-one stood in judgement of me over where I had been or where I was and it was reassuring that I could be a mess and still be loved. It was during that time that I began meeting regularly for bible study with Pastor John I slowly grew in confidence to stretch out a bit more. During our 1-2-1 meetings I was able to talk a lot about the difficulties I faced daily without feeling judged. It was refreshing to have a place where I could be honest and with it came a greater sense of freedom. I knew that my meetings would not act as a miracle cure, but they certainly helped facilitate progress and with each passing week I felt a growing sense of a desire for Jesus to return in my heart. I began to feel alive in worship and would openly give praise to God for His grace and mercy. Instead of running away at the end of each service, I would stay and have tea with the other members as we would chat about various things. What once were strangers in a crowd had changed to become familiar faces and a new family, and I really started to love being with them every week. I got more and more involved in the church, joining group courses, working in youth ministry and other activities of service. It gave me a sense of purpose as I began growing in my knowledge and understanding of God and His son Jesus. It also helped divert my focus away from 'Everything'. I began wanting to know more and more and so I began with a commitment every day to reading the bible and listening to an audio version. I became so involved in my desire to know God more that I could no longer go a day without spending some time in devotional prayer. I began to fall in love with The Word and learning about Jesus, and I began to see quote of scripture from The Bible realised in my daily life.

However I would still think of 'Everything' and missed him terribly if I allowed myself to spend too much time in a thought over him, but as the months went on, it got easier as my focus continued to shift from him onto God. There were moments when I would catch myself during the day somewhat surprised after realising that I had not spent any time mourning 'Everything' (which had been my daily ritual) and then feeling a sense of accomplishment over my growing focus on God. I knew and accepted the pain had not completely gone as I was still not over him or the loss of my relationship which I had placed so much hope and trust in, but I was in a new place where I allowed God to be my strength and turned to Him whenever I struggled to cope and with that my prayers also began to change. Whilst I continued to pray for 'Everything' daily, I stopped praying for his return. I knew that it was no longer healthy for me to continue on in a desire for him whilst I was trying to focus on receiving more of Christ. I realised that the two concepts could not mix and were simply like oil and water. I knew that I had to put down the thoughts which lead me to overly concern myself with thoughts of 'Everything' and his wellbeing. I had to take captive the thoughts that would run through my mind and into my heart of me being back in his arms. I had to replace him with thoughts that only produced a positive outcome by focusing on God's Word and the promises it yielded for my future, but it was hard as I still had to battle with myself and my inability to fully let go. There was still a part of me that wanted to remain in hope for 'Everything' purely because of what I had always believed of who he was to me when I first met him. The truth was he was no longer that person and neither was I the same woman. He and I at one stage had both thought we wanted certain things from each other and life, but our plans changed and no longer included one another; something had crossed over and I could no longer look back. It was time to embrace the uncertain future with my eyes wide open and firmly fixed on Christ.

I had begun to take many steps towards deepening my faith through intimacy with God and by the time I was ready to be baptised it felt as if I had cruised into fifth gear in my relationship with The Father. Not only that, but I was finally reaching for a place of peace and for once life started to feel that bit easier. The burdens were lifting and I was beginning to smile again from the inside out. I reflected on how far I had come, knowing that this time my motives were right. I loved God with all that I had, and it was an uncompromising love unlike in the past where I placed 'Everything' in the driving seat of my heart. I knew with a clear mind that I could go forward and be baptised with an understanding of what I was doing and why and with a vision of being in the arms of Christ, not that of a man's. I longed for nothing more than to see my dreams realised, but mostly to finally give God a part of me that I had always kept away hidden in secret.

The truth was that initially when I had first met 'Everything' and wanted to explore the possibilities of a new life in Christ; whilst I felt a real difference once I stepped over the threshold and began to live my life seeking God, there was also an ever present desire to gain love and some sense of approval from 'Everything'. There was a part of me that was seeking after his heart which meant that I could never truly ever seek after God. I raced into it all head first, thinking that once I gained the love of my man then and only then would I need deal with God's business, but I was wrong. On reflection I finally got the real reason why previous attempts at baptism had failed. It wasn't because of circumstances beyond my control with 'Everything' firstly becoming ill and then the church removing me as a candidate. It was because God knew my heart carried a goal that was not Christ seeking. Yes, I was growing as a Christian, but there was always a part of me that placed limits on The Father – a place where I held up a very evident stop sign. There were times when I genuinely believed in my actions toward God as being genuine, but whilst I was seeking more of God and I did love Him, He was not my only reason for wanting to be baptised. As a result, it was impossible to please God or step into the real light of the Holy Spirit until I was cleansed of my sinful desires, so that the blessings of accepting Christ could be realised. It even went deeper; throughout my journey over the previous three years I had constantly battled with disobedience and not listening to the warning signs from The Father. Every time I was faced with a conviction over certain choices in my relationship with 'Everything' I chose to ignore it. I always knew that I had to make a change which reflected God as priority but I could never bring myself to do it for fear of losing the man I loved and it was only until I was stripped bare....naked of all that I had clung to, that God could shape and mould me into the masterpiece he had always planned. It was being stripped and vulnerable which finally forced me to accept my mistakes, grow and learn, and to lean on the only man that should have ever possessed my heart, and that was the man that was Jesus Christ who died to give me life and set me free. And I was free. Finally free from a life that yielded my walk around barren wasteland. I had found my way out through trusting in God through faith in the uncertain.

The morning of my baptism brought on the same all too familiar pondering over my decision to openly give my life to Christ once again. I was pensive in anticipation over the journey I was about to embark upon and for a moment questioned if I was truly ready or even good enough. I sat in my home alone again, but in the stillness of the atmosphere which had previously yielded such sadness, I felt the peaceful presence of the Holy Spirit telling me that indeed it was time and that in fact I was ready. I smiled and breathed a sigh of relief as I exhaled deeply. The road had been long, but this time there were no obstacles ahead of me and nothing to stop me walking along my path to freedom. I was no longer afraid, but the thought of continuing on in my journey without 'Everything' felt as if a small part of me was still missing. Although there had been so much pain and times when I had prayed to God in regret of meeting 'Everything', in that moment I was nothing but appreciative for who he had been in my life and I wished that he could have been there to witness the end result of a struggle which led to finishing the race, but despite the longing I felt something bigger than 'Everything' and a real desire to press on towards gaining my prize, and in that moment of clarity came a growing excitement in anticipation for my future life in Christ. What had come to pass no longer mattered. The past no longer matter and no longer did it have any control over me. God had shown me so much grace and favour. He had taken me and had begun to transform me from the inside out. It had been a long and steady progress, with much resistance at times on my part, but I was moving and with that He continued to pour blessings over my life. Despite the chapter of 'Everything' being over, I had all that I ever needed and wanted and for the first time since the breakup I actually felt truly at peace.

When I arrived at church I felt suddenly caught up in a whirlwind of hustle and bustle; children ran around excitedly and members of the congregation quickly shuffled to and fro in anticipation of the ceremony. I felt overwhelmed with happiness as I saw the faces of friends who did not regularly attend church, but were there to support me. Adrenaline began to rush through my body as my heartbeat quickened in pace. I started to feel a sense of nervousness as I tied up my hair and removed my shoes. I had decided on wearing a long white tunic, but coupled it with a black top and leggings to go underneath so that my modesty would be kept intact after emerging from the water. I looked in the bathroom mirror as to compose myself for the impending ceremony and as I stood there looking at my reflection, I saw something different. The woman who stared back at me no longer seemed ashamed of who she was but had come to accept what stood before her and as I stood there looking directly into the reflection of my own eyes I paused in the moment and for the first time I didn't avoid my myself or try to look away quickly. It was almost as if I were finally accepting and recognising who I was, and in that moment, I realised that the acceptance of my reflection was a representation of an acceptance of God's perfect love and will for my life.

The ceremony was filled with praise and worship where I was able to freely dance, sing, rejoice and give thanks with the other baptismal candidates. This was followed up by the giving of our testimonies. I had not prepared a speech but I knew that I wanted to share with the congregation who I was and where I had been with honesty and integrity. I knew that the vast majority of my Christian brothers and sisters at the fellowship church knew very little about me other than seeing a broken woman who used to attend and sit at the back of the church in tears. I wanted them to know of my growing strength and courage in God as a way to encourage others who may have felt some of the emotions and struggles I had experienced. I stood there not sure what I would say, but I knew that whatever I said would be just right because it was my truth. More importantly, I knew that the Holy Spirit would guide me so I had nothing to fear, and out of my mouth came the story. As I spoke, I looked around at the faces of those whose gazes were locked in deep concentration listening to what I had to say. I remained focused, not straying from the point, but as my words expressed a deepening of emotions, I looked at my best friend Amiyah of 32 years and as our eyes connected, I began to cry. I knew that as soon as I looked at her, being one of my biggest supporters and one of the very few people who had been by my side through it all, I wouldn't have been able to hold back the tears but as I finished off and got ready to enter the water, a sense of happiness returned.

As I slowly walked down the steps and into the baptismal pool surrounded by the congregation, I gave one last thought to that of 'Everything' and in a quick flashback over the previous three years of my life I felt emotional. I finally realised the true purpose of the role he had played in my life. Perhaps it wasn't to have walked by my side into forever as my husband, but to be a vessel in order to help facilitate my walk with Christ and to bring me back into The Father's arms. I finally understood the true reasoning for and the depth of my desire toward him; he was like the fragrance of lilies in a field, the view of a valley on a mountain top and the lapping of waves against the shore, but it was never him….it was God. I had never understood in the past why a man who came from such humble beginnings created such a pull of great magnitude in my heart. It came with seemingly effortless mannerisms and wisdom, but it was the Christ like essence within 'Everything' that reached into the very depth of my soul and with it I gave thanks to God for his life and what 'Everything' had done for me in mine. I smiled whole heartedly as I took one last step down to the pool and into the arms of Pastor John and an elder of the church. I was ready. I stood there with eyes closed and my arms across my chest, listening to the guiding voice of Pastor John as he lead with words confirming a confession of my faith in Christ as I was about to be baptised. Then there was a pause and a free falling sensation as the water engulfed me and I went under. I felt weightless as the sound of the water churned and gurgled around me, and before I could even assess what was happening under the surface, I was back up and out of the water to the cheers of friends and family as my baptism was confirmed. As I wiped the water from my eyes, I jigged about up and down like a child in the excitement over what I had just done. As I took each step up and back out of the pool dripping with water and feeling somewhat cold, I did my own little victory dance and an overwhelming sense of winning came over me. I no longer felt cold, but on fire and all I wanted to do was dance. I still felt like myself, but instead of the older more complicated woman, a new and much better version. It felt like my old coat of guilt and condemnation had been taken off and replaced with the finest coat made of freedom and redemption. I was home, and although I didn't quite know where the next step lead to on the pathway of my life, I knew that Christ was right there by my side every step of the way until I walked home to heaven.

All of a sudden, I felt overwhelmed with tiredness and I wanted to go home and rest. I fell into a state of real calm to the point of weakness and with it came an immediate need to be alone with God, and so I made my way back home. As I walked up the stairs and back into the silence of my surroundings, I placed myself into the hands of The Father and lay there quietly on my sofa being soothed by the Holy Spirit. No more needed to be said; just a need to receive His peace and so I remained in the presence of His sanctuary but despite it all, there was still a small part of me that propelled my thoughts back toward 'Everything' wishing that he had been there to witness my baptism. There was still a very evident part of the picture which I felt had been missing from the day and it was him. Somehow it still felt as if he was the missing piece to the jigsaw puzzle of my very existence. However I knew that with God's help I was going to work it all out and that I wasn't going to be alone again.

CHAPTER 14

Alone Again

It was New Year's Eve and a time of reflection as I looked back over the years' three hundred and sixty five day life cycle which had flown by seemingly as quickly as if it were three hundred and sixty five minutes. So many things had happened that symbolised change, but the change in time had certainly not yielded the much needed healing in my heart that I had hoped for. Despite my baptism the month before and a greater sense of peace, I still felt incomplete and questioned if life would ever truly feel better on a consistent basis or if I would finally make it to a place of victory with the past life of 'Everything' finally being behind me for good. I was frustrated within myself for seemingly being stuck in a never ending whirlpool of nostalgia. I did not want to love him anymore, but still I was trapped by the strength of my emotional pull toward him. It was difficult to understand how I could love and hurt so much with equal measure, but close friends encouraged me by letting me know that my feelings were normal and that I was to trust the process. It felt irrational and somewhat crazy to still feel as strongly then as I did from the very beginning for a man who had moved on and not looked back, but I couldn't help how I felt. I also struggled with accepting that he was no longer mine and I greatly battled with the idea of him loving another woman, but whether it was a reality or not, I knew I had to work on forgetting about 'Everything' and focus on Jesus who had been the one and only constant source of unconditional love from the very beginning even if I hadn't realised it. I tried so hard to make a fresh start and move on, but the problem was that 'Everything' was a constant reminder in all aspects of my everyday life. His name was the passwords for most of my accounts and logins, his DVD and gaming collection were all around the apartment, his post was still being received at our home, his clothes still remained in the wardrobe with his shoes still under our bed, but the biggest reminder of all was through my relationship with God. Each time I lifted my voice in prayer there too was 'Everything' in my thoughts. As much as I was a woman of a mature enough age and of sound mind, I was still just that…a woman and so I was still highly connected with my emotions. I would repeatedly look over old pictures which reflected a more loving time between us, and as I connected with the images of love I would kiss them in floods of tears as I said my goodnights to 'Everything' and then wrap myself up in one of his old T-shirts as I went to bed, just to feel a sense of closeness to him. It had been a number of weeks since accepting Jesus Christ as my Lord and Saviour through baptism, but I was still left with a longing and a sense of sadness and regret as I acknowledged that it had been four whole months since the breakup and I had not seen 'Everything' for a considerable amount of time during those months apart. I couldn't believe how quickly the time had gone by but not the pain. The anxiety and sense of abandonment was still as raw as if 'Everything' had said goodbye for the final time just the day before. I thought about where I should be emotionally – getting over it and moving on, but still I was in a complete state of bereavement. Although I had slowly begun to accept with a heavy heart that 'Everything' had moved on and we would never get back together, I still missed the man who had been my best friend over the previous three years of my life, but missing him yielded very little prospect, as we had grown so distant from each other that I couldn't even reach out to him as the trusted and reliable friend he had always been to me in time of need. I desperately wanted to but I knew that if I were to make contact with him it would not help and only serve to prolong the difficulties I was trying to conquer in an acceptance of moving on.

Not only did the impending New Year mark a significant change in reflection of all that was happening in my life, but it also marked the end of our contract on the apartment we had shared and so I too was finally taking those steps and moving out of the home we had previously tried to build together. Although

'Everything' had already moved out sometime before, the majority of his belongings still remained and with it a continuous feeling of nostalgia in the atmosphere. I looked around the flat gazing carefully over all of our possessions which we had built up in capacity during the years of our relationship and I realised with some astonishment that we had actually created a significant life together, but the significance was no longer relevant as our possessions had to be separated and bagged up for transportation to a future in very different locations. As I took a deep breath, gathering strength in preparation for the task at hand, I began the process of packing and labelling individual boxes with either his name on them or mine but then I stopped as I fell into a moment of weakness. I couldn't do it. It felt like torture having to fold away his favourite items of clothing, computer games and other personal effects. It was as if I were being forced to face the end of my relationship all over again, but this time having to face saying goodbye for one very last and final time. I stood there motionless and as I did so, the emotional burden hit me so hard that all I could do was tilt my head back and squeeze my eyes shut as I tried to focus away the tears. Slowly, I opened my eyes still looking up to the ceiling as if I were waiting for The Father to whisk me away from my pain, but instead I just remained standing there hanging almost lifeless. I felt stretched to my emotional capacity and wasn't sure if I could actually take any more of the turmoil before snapping for good. Whilst I knew that the Holy Spirit was with me, I also knew that my struggles were very real and had not just evaporated since affirming my faith by being baptised and having that deeper relationship with God through Jesus Christ. I was still a woman who had very evident fears and insecurities which I was working through and the loss of 'Everything' greatly impacted upon that. However, I still had some level of peace and a firm place that I knew I could go to when I felt a moment of weakness and loneliness and that was in God, because through it all and despite how I was feeling at the time, it was evident that The Father was still there nurturing, directing and supporting me with due love, care and attention.

In that very moment of sadness, I stretched out my arms in prayer and asked The Father to strengthen me. I didn't know if I could carry on with packing up the various items as it felt tiring and burdensome. I felt as if I were being forced to face all of the memories from the relationship as box by box, I closed another chapter of my life with 'Everything'. Nevertheless, The Father being true to His promises strengthened me enough to clear my mind to find the focus needed to continue on slowly. The packing allowed me to begin setting 'Everything' free item by item and bit by bit, despite the heaviness of my circumstances. I was still awash with tears, but as I continued to put each individual item away focusing on God's peace and light I felt a sense of joy and positive reflection come over me as slowly I begun to let it all go. In that moment I thanked God for a beautiful time in my life, but could only breathe out a faint prayer of some acceptance in acknowledging that the

time had reached the end of its cycle. My thoughts turned to
'Everything' as I wondered where he might be at that very moment
and I desperately hoped that he had found his way to church, as
we had always gone to a service on New Year's Eve to see in and
celebrate the New Year in with Our Lord. I smiled at the very
memory and although I was not with him, I knew that whatever
choice he had made that night God was with him and that gave me
comfort. There was never a moment when God had let either one
of us go and I knew that The Father was holding on to me at that
time, particularly with a firm grip. There was no mistaking that
through it all He was there and that the Holy Spirit was guiding me
through the wilderness. Despite my pain, I knew that something
was changing in me for the better in a way I had not fully yet
accepted. I struggled, but in my struggles Father God was laying a
strong foundation for something else to come which far surpassed
my understanding. Although I sensed an idea of a greater plan I
wasn't there yet in a place of acceptance and so I still struggled with
feeling alone in the physical, but in the supernatural something was
definitely changing.

As I continued packing bags and boxes I wiped away my
tears in an effort to reclaim my sense of control through focusing
on Jesus' love. I went back to thinking about time and how much
of it I had recently spent in mourning and how broken I had been
for what seemed like an indeterminate period of time. I continued
on to acknowledge that with the loving help and guidance from
Christ, I needed to make significant changes in order to really move

forward. I already felt as if too much time had been stolen from me and although I could never get that lost time back, I knew that it was never too late for a fresh start. Just a few months before I had begun working in counsel with Pastor John to help get myself back on track in an attempt to live out the joy in my life the way in which God had intended for me and to replace the sadness with happiness. I had already begun to grow in my relationship with God, resulting in finally becoming baptised and I was beginning to fall in love with Jesus that bit more day by day. I was making steady progress and coming through to a real sense of breaking through my chains and being set free, but in a moment of weakness during the packing up of our belongings and with the reality of moving away from and toward a separate direction to that of 'Everything,' there was a growing sense of anguish and the churning up of even more challenges. I didn't expect to feel the weighty emotions of regret and sadness return; I had already gone through it and certainly did not want to relive it. I had already cried and wept and I had already gone over things in my mind to reconcile and reach what I thought was a turning point. I did not want to go through it all over again even if just to reflect in a moment and I certainly did not want to take the pain of the past year into the new one, so I made a decision right there in that moment. I made a promise to myself that I was going to give all of my fears, woes, anxieties and insecurities over to God and allow Him to work on 'Everything'. I was going to release him to The Father in trust and faith because I could no longer reconcile anything by my strength and in knowing the possibilities through Christ, I allowed for the miraculous to take place in the supernatural. The only responsibility I could take at that time was for who I was and as I acknowledged that fact, I decided to shake off my blues and go to church as I had always done on the eve of a new year and saw in the first day of the rest of my life with God the Father.

The beginning of the New Year saw in a changed attitude and approach to how I was going to move forward in my life however, it didn't last very long. Ongoing fear meant that I still limited God through my lack of belief and faith that He was working my life out in order to achieve the very best result. I wasn't fully giving Him credit for the very evident fact that He was working on me, ironing out all of the kinks which had been a continuous stumbling block during my relationship with Him. I had forgotten just how much I had not only survived but how much I had grown since allowing God to take the driver's seat, but in a moment of weakness I took a number of steps backwards which threw me off course. Initially all was fine. I had found and moved into my own new home and along with a renewed sense of achieving what had felt like the impossible I went on living my life feeling joyful and hopeful. The future felt bright and full of fresh promise as I mentally felt as if I were cruising into fifth gear. I would spend lengthy time in devotional learning and prayer and for the first time in my Christian walk I felt God speak directly to me. The sound of His voice was strong and clear and His confirmation left no doubt in my mind of what I could expect in the future. The day God spoke to me His powerful but gentle voice left me with no questioning of who had spoken, and the sheer connection and magnitude of it brought me to tears. Humbled and comforted, I thanked God for His confirmation and dedication to continue on with what He had promised and it gave me what I thought was a clear indication of what was soon to come, but I was wrong.

I believed that I had heard God promise me 'Everything' and whilst I no longer saw or spoke to him on a regular basis after we parted ways to carry on living our individual lives, I kept him faithfully in prayer especially after I had felt God had spoken into my heart so clearly. I had always been hopeful of reconciliation and would pray for the safe keeping of 'Everything' and for him to really accept God's will for his life which I believed included me. I prayed for this with great diligence, not realising that I was somewhat taking away the focus from myself and my own spiritual development and placing it back on 'Everything' once again. I continued to believe in faith that by God's promise I formed a determinate part of his life plan. I also knew that the process of waiting was not going to be easy and that I would have to exercise the greatest amount of trust and faith in God's timing whilst The Father worked on building and preparing both of His children for the lives He had intended for us. Not only that, but the waiting and then outcome was going to be on His timing and during that time I needed to live in obedience to His will. During the initial time of waiting there was a shift in which 'Everything' and I grew in more regular contact and during that time we were much kinder and friendlier toward each other. Although at that point I never revealed the true extent of my feelings towards 'Everything' and I continued to act seemingly neutral in his presence, I continued on remaining calm but heavily focused in prayer to God for the reconciliation I so eagerly desired. As I became more confident and excited about the possibility of God's promise being on the horizon, there was an awkward shift and something changed drastically leaving all of my hopes dashed to pieces. The diversion in plan came as soon as I became impatient in waiting on God. Although it had only been a very short time since I had heard God's voice of promise, I had begun to feel the pressure of the separation believing that too much actual time was starting to build up creating further distance between us. It had been a growing number of months in which 'Everything' and I had been apart and so I became convinced that any reconciliation had become irretrievable, unobtainable and borderline impossible especially as 'Everything' was showing no real signs of wanting to get back together and re-enter a relationship with me. In fairness, up until that point I had also remained seemingly platonic, but on the inside of my emotions screamed a very present and continuing love that would not quit. My focus on God and waiting on His leadership began to grow shaky as I grew more and more impatient and steadily I began to question His timing. It seemed to me as if nothing were happening, and at that stage the waiting started to feel like a game I no longer wanted to play. I began questioning what I was waiting for and if I actually needed to wait for an obvious sign from God or an actual instruction. I toyed with the idea that it was time to take some action and do something about it all. I felt confused and began to grow in greater frustration. I continued to pray, but there was a developing war in my mind and I felt as if I needed to take some sort of action in finding out what was going on with 'Everything'. I knew that I had not yet nearly exercised enough of a significant amount of trust in God which should have been limitless and in needing to work things out I determined that the waiting had been too long and I needed to seek my own answers. I sensed in my spirit that any choice in taking action to seek out 'Everything' without God's say so was not wise at the time, but I still battled with disobedience because I wanted to see an immediate result. I felt a need for control which I had always battled with all the way through my relationship with 'Everything' and also through my Christian walk which had again reared its ugly head, but still I was unwilling to compromise. I hadn't anticipated that I was being distracted by my feelings which were causing me to lose focus and consider other options which were not conducive to the will of God. Nevertheless I rationalised that there was a part of the process which involved my partaking of action and, fired up with fuel of the enemy, I made a choice to tell 'Everything' how I was feeling but the reaction was not one which I had hoped for. Whilst I did not expect him to run back to me with open arms in that very moment because there were still things which needed to be worked upon, I still had an expectation that he would say he still had feelings for me and that he had missed me, but he didn't. Much like the very first night in question over marriage, he refused to talk about anything involving how he felt as he claimed he did not think that what he had to say would help me in moving forward and in those very words, once again I felt crushed.

I walked away from 'Everything' feeling that I had been foolish. After all, why would he want to reconcile with me after ceremoniously leaving all those months before. I had been unrealistic, leaving my head in the clouds for a minute whilst seemingly becoming detached from any reality. Perhaps it was the ignorance in a lack of acceptance which had kept me in a futile position. The love had gone and was replaced by his desire to move on separately whilst I remained in a fool's paradise of imagination but not reality. The problem was that in knowing his feelings for me were a very evident null and void, there seemed to be a change in my whole dynamics and suddenly the atmosphere to my very existence shifted. Once again life felt bland, tasteless and lifeless. I could no longer feel the elements of my life being a blank canvas of a fresh start, but something that lacked texture and depth. I felt alone again….truly alone. The hopes and aspirations which I had held onto in believing that 'Everything' simply needed some time to himself to discover who he was, were dashed as I began to accept that he hadn't just left for a short period of time to experience new pastures only to realise where it was greenest and return home, he had gone for good.

In that moment I reflected on God's promise and felt confused over His voice which I had believed to have heard very clearly not long before. The truth was that I had in-fact heard from God, but quite possibly there was an error in my interpretation. I battled with thinking that God had gone back on His promise, but it was not that The Father had done so – more so that I had made assumptions on His timing and direction. Once again I had allowed my ego to get in the way, taking away His control and as I drove home I acknowledged my failings and felt an all too familiar mind-set that placed me in a prison of regret. I felt chained to my apparent mistakes and with that I felt consumed by intense pain once more. This time it was very real…more real than it had ever been before. There was no mistaking the fact that 'Everything' was clear in his intentions towards me because I felt a distinct difference in his presence. It was platonic and there was no emotion behind his words. I felt wracked with a sense of overwhelming sorrow as I visualised the man I once knew who had always loved me from the very beginning, knowing that he no longer existed in my future. It was evident that he was replaced with the new man who although he walked and talked like 'Everything' was no longer the person I knew. He had changed and outgrown his need and love for me through his various experiences since the end of our relationship and despite a promise I could see no way for God to restore anything between us.

The following weeks I descended back into a place of mourning, confusion, and a battle with acceptance and abandonment, but this time it felt worse because there was no mistaking the truth of his words. My ability to cope was made worse when it became evident that 'Everything' and rightly so, was getting on with his life. It was made harder by fact that he seemed really happy whilst my life without him descended further into chaos. I watched silently at a distance looking at status updates and photos on social media which reflected a life of purpose, drive and freedom whilst my life was the complete opposite. During this time there was something inexplicably different about the difficulties I encountered after confessing my continued feelings for 'Everything' which left me paralysed emotionally. Somehow, at the peak of our breakup months before, I had been able to focus on giving my excruciating pain over to God allowing Him to take full control. It was the hardest thing I ever had to do, but in it and at the time I found liberation because I felt a touch from The Father and an ever present hand on my life in spite of not knowing where I was going or where I would end up. However, this time there was a change in the direction and I no longer felt touched by that gentle unseen guidance. It felt as if God's hand which had previously been held out for hope was the very same hand which had allowed me to fall. It seemed as if God was exercising discipline to borderline punishment and so the sheer nature of its vigour left me in a state of utter devastation and I couldn't understand why.

There was a period of some weeks where I did not want to see anyone nor did I pray. I just wanted to be alone again. I felt as if there was no-one who could understand or help me and I no longer had faith that God truly loved me. I spent most days lying on my sofa lost in my thoughts of abandonment whilst watching mythical movies like The Lord of the Rings to escape my reality. Whilst I thought about 'Everything' my focus was mostly towards God as I confessed bitterness in my heart towards His lack of doing in my life. I shouted and screamed and then became quiet, point blank refusing to acknowledge God. I refused to spend any time in devotional learning or prayer in my defiance of Him, and it wasn't long before I felt a continuing darkness over my mind and a sense of losing control. Nonetheless the darkness, although hovering and ready to consume me, became less of a threat as my heart began to soften again towards The Father. Despite it all I knew better and I acknowledged that whilst I didn't feel any victory in that moment, I had still moved forward and made a great amount of progress since the breakup despite some level of back sliding. I knew that although I felt alone I was not alone, and so again I had to claim control over my thoughts and actions with the help of the Holy Spirit. I recognised that the enemy was trying to distract me with thoughts of irrationality, lies and sin in an attempt to get me to consider other options, as I thought about meeting up with an ex-boyfriend for some sort of companionship. Luckily I saw the attempts for what they were and rejected them despite still wanting to heavily sedate my emotional turmoil. Still, God was moving and saw my needs and so He sent someone unexpected to help me. It was Andrew; a mutual friend of mine and 'Everything' who I had previously believed had not liked me, but out of the blue there he was. Andrew was a pillar of strength, solid in his words and committed to supporting me. He seemed to truly understand my struggles and so each day he would send me a message telling me to wake up (emotionally speaking), followed by inspirational quotes or images that gave me great comfort, direction and the ability to face the days ahead. Andrew never allowed me to lose focus and whenever I became unstable, there he was to pick me back up again with a word or a shoulder to cry on. When he stepped into my life to seemingly help bridge the gap so I could cross back into a place of peace, he was my first encounter of and a true understanding of how God uses the most unexpected and seemingly inappropriate people as vessels of light. It was as if Andrew had rescued me from the brink of insanity with a direct but caring approach, and I learnt the importance of what it meant to be a support and encourager to those in times of need. He taught me how to be a strong tower, and I began to understand a deep sense of purpose in helping others as I had been blessed to find refuge in my own Good Samaritan. As I began to feel more positive through his friendship and although his approach was very different, Andrew taught me a valuable lesson in remaining focused and letting go of the things I could not change. He encouraged me to build on the new, starting with myself by not mourning something that was no longer real or relevant in my own personal journey, but mostly he was a calming influence in the midst of my chaos. I acknowledged the importance of coming alongside someone in need and recognised that my own friend

Andrew, and Good Samaritan had not only come into my life to awaken me from stasis, but as a means to help me rise up in my spirit and to remind me that I could never ever be alone again and was always loved.

It was true that God loved me but the enemy also wanted to destroy me and so I found myself continuing on in a battle despite the help of Andrew, my friend and Good Samaritan. There were periods of time where I would feel so encouraged that I felt as if nothing could break me down, but then out of the blue the simplest reminder of 'Everything' had me back in a place of sadness. I knew that I could never win back his love, but I still imagined a life which could have been. There were nights when I would dream of 'Everything' where I visualised him walking with me holding my hand and, in the morning upon waking, I would pray to God for the opportunity to walk with 'Everything' in real life as I had done so in my dreams. Although the opportunity never came there was something in me that believed it might still be possible, but the important thing at that time was to let it go and let God in and so I pressed forward and began to focus on my Father. I threw myself into church ministry, praying and learning the word and once again things began to feel easier. Despite the ups and downs there was a real a sense of purpose in my life although I could not identify what exactly God was doing with me, still I knew intuitively He was building me up for something good but in the blink of an eye my life changed again.

I woke up one morning feeling a real sense of indifference and confused as to why I felt as though I had lost motivation. The weather was dull and although it was the middle of summer, there was a real chill in the atmosphere. As I got ready for work I couldn't seem to lift what became a very evident heaviness and so I prayed for God to lift it, but still I remained confused and uncertain but I did not know what that 'something' was that I felt uncertain about. Later that morning, I left home in the direction of work jumping in my car to make my way to the train station. As I parked up and began walking, I realised that 'Everything' was still there; in my mind, in my thoughts, in my very being. I had seen him a few days earlier and it was still very evident within me that I was not yet over him. As I stepped out to cross the road, the echoes of my mind began to sound like clashing symbols as I was reminded all over again of a lost love and before I knew it, I heard the sound of a car horn. Suddenly I felt a crack of pain surge through my ankle which transcended to my leg and then straight up to my hips, and then I was face down on the ground. I was unable to move; my body was reeling in agony as I realised I had been hit by a car. The pain was so intense I could not determine the source and as I lay there I began to cry in panic. I did not know what was happening; all I knew was that I lay in the middle of the street physically damaged, broken and alone, which also reflected what I had felt emotionally. I could do nothing but wait for help. As I cried out in agony over the growing pain in my body, a growing sense of fear and panic swept over me.

I lay there for what felt like hours as passers-by tried to help by calling the emergency services and my mum. I was cold, but the coldness was overshadowed by pain. I sobbed heartfelt tears as a kind lady held my hand whilst waiting for the ambulance to arrive and another lady covered me with her scarf to help keep me warm whilst I begged them not to leave me. There were a number of thoughts that raced through my mind, but one very dominant thought was 'Everything'. I was scared and in that moment of fear I wanted him to be there, but I also knew he couldn't be because he was no longer responsible for my support and rescue. As the ambulance service asked questions on their arrival, checked me over and then gave me gas and air to help relieve the pain, suddenly my mind floated away from all that was going on and on to God. I knew that He had saved my life and protected me from something far worse happening in the accident and there was no-one – not even 'Everything' that could have rescued me in that moment. I imagined that God had sent an angel to protect me and through the haze of pain relief I remained in the comfort of His light. By the time I had been transported to the hospital, checked in and left to wait alone in a wheelchair in A&E, the pain relief began to wear off as the pain returned in growing intensity. I sat there trying to shift myself in the wheelchair to help shift the discomfort, but the more I tried to move the more intense the pain felt. Defeated, I sat back, remained still and called out to God. I acknowledged to Him that I had spent so much time in mourning a lost love, I had missed the very love He had for me through Jesus Christ who was my saviour and I felt a sense of His sadness as He explained how long He had tried to gain my full attention. I knew that I had to try harder and so I asked God with intention and made a promise that if He would find it in His heart to heal me of my physical pain and injuries, I would dedicate my life to Him without compromise.

Initially and straight after the accident my injuries didn't seem to be quite as bad as originally diagnosed. Although I was left with my foot broken along with nerve damage in my ankle, the recovery period was estimated at just a few weeks. However, as the first week finished my mobility lessened and the pain continued to grow in strength and with it I forgot what I had promised God as I fell into depression. Simple tasks of being able to brush my teeth, shower or reach for food items in the fridge became impossible without the assistance of friends and family. It was also hard for me to accept the help offered by those closest to me as my fierce independence coupled with not wanting to inconvenience anyone made me push people away. As a result I sank into despair and once again my prayer life and any devotional time with God became non-existent. My distraction wasn't because I did not want to be close with The Father but simply because I became overwhelmed, focusing on my injuries which were increasingly impacting on my life. Consultants confirmed on further investigation, that my foot was damaged in multiple places which meant my rehabilitation would be more extensive than originally anticipated. I became frustrated as I wanted to get back to some normality which involved my every day activities, instead of being forced day in day out to be left alone with my oppressive feelings. Try as I might, once again I felt as if I were fighting a losing battle. It seemed as if each and every time I had tried to move on and forward in my life there would be something to knock me back down to zero. It was then that I began reading the Book of Job in an attempt to find some encouragement but I could do nothing to apply the words I read to my own life because I did not fully understand the book's message. All I could understand was that Job was a man who had gone through and endured great suffering despite his love for God and so I concluded that I too was going to have to continue on to experience much more suffering before a final breakthrough, if ever.

I wanted to trust in God but I felt weak and unsure if I would ever really have the ability to stand firm in fear.

CHAPTER 15

Standing Firm in Fear

It had been well over a month since my accident with very little progress to my healing. I was frustrated and out of my comfort zone because of the many adjustments I had to make to my life, including being unable to walk anywhere without the assistance of crutches. Even normal tasks like taking a shower were difficult as I struggled to get in to stand in the cubicle. I felt stripped of my dignity each time I would try to do something without using the crutches, and would cry as I struggled to walk independently without success. As I sat there with tears streaming down my face, I listened to the words of the worship music playing in the background in an attempt to seek comfort. I could hear the lyrics of how lovely, worthy and wonderful God had always been and as I listened to each of the words the tears continued but the feelings began to change for the better as I realised that God had always been as such to me. The overwhelming feeling of fear began turning into some outward peace and the heightened state of resistance caused by panic turned to calm, and as my emotions shifted, trying desperately to settle, I felt a deeper sense of God's presence and comfort. He was reassuring me telling me not to be afraid because He was present and would see His work in my life through to completion. I could sense Him saying to hold steadfast and be courageous as He asked me to receive His healing and to allow Him in. I knew that God did not want me to feel alone, but I still struggled with bringing myself to allow Him in taking full control over my life even after so much time in a deepening relationship and understanding of The Father because I did not know how to. I wanted to reach out and take God's hand but I couldn't move nor could I let go of myself and as I sat hunched forward, I exhaled sobbing through my tears. In that very moment, it felt as if I were the only person in the world feeling as desperately as I did and whilst this was not true because all suffer at some stage through life, the powerful feeling of loneliness continued to retain a hold over me. I couldn't face letting go because letting go was alien to me, so instead I continued to sob with my face buried deep within my hands. Reverting back to type, I felt as if I were never going to be able to look up from that very moment into any form of recovery because the sadness and pain were too heavy to ever shift even in the depth of understanding the extent of The Father's love. Nevertheless in some weird way holding on to my pain was unintentionally giving me some degree of comfort. It was all I had ever known and I immediately recognised the pattern as type, as its familiarity made it all bearable. Despite the ever growing painful mistakes of my life, through it all they were mine and in my mind at least I had something in my desperate situation. I still struggled greatly from day to day with truly believing that God loved me enough to do the unimaginable and seemingly unobtainable in my life because deep down I felt I did not deserve it. I felt as if I were a mess and a failure because still I was struggling with God's lesson which demonstrated my need to trust in Him. It was as simple as that, but the victim in me could not understand the link between trust, surrender and freedom. I felt ugly once again and had fallen into reclaiming previous strongholds in my mind as I fell into the temptation of thinking independently of God. My mind continued on in an act of thinking ungrateful thoughts as I continued on in believing that God's work in me was futile despite His love for me. I struggled to accept that God could ever love me unconditionally because I never knew of an unconditional love. I had always felt rejected and abandoned. I felt like a loser and definitely incapable of being a vessel for God to do much with. In my mind I was a sad and destitute woman who had no clue what to do in life. I had no longer felt any sense of purpose and value and could not see what God could possibly do through me. I also battled with questioning why would He take care of me as a father would his child?

There was nothing to convince me of anything different. I never had a father as a parent I could really trust. My dad left me when I was a teenager; he walked away from me to pursue his own life by moving to Jamaica and never looked back. Before he left, I had never really known him. My earliest memories of my dad were of a man who was a tall, dark stranger with large eyes. That is all. He never smiled and he certainly never hugged me; just collected me from my mother and dropped me off at the front door of my grandma's house every other weekend or so like a parcel delivery man. I never saw him and I hardly ever spoke to him. His voice was that of a stranger to me. I formed no relationship and no attachment with him. It felt as if he was someone standing way out in the distance – unreachable and unavailable, and that became normal and accepted. And because I formed no bond with my biological father, I did not know what it meant to have a father's love. It also meant that because I did not have a dominant male presence in my life, I did not know what a solid relationship with a man truly was or what it actually looked or felt like, and so my relationships with men became distorted. I formed my own opinion on how these relationships should be – often without success. I reached for my own rule book of life where men were concerned and as a result it ended in many failed relationships with each one taking away another piece of my trust and confidence with it. This in turn meant that I did not know how to trust or rely on the one father figure that knew me before I was formed. That being God the Father.

I never truly knew a male figure that did not judge me or one that would not give up on me. I never truly knew a male figure that I could show my vulnerability to, fail in front of or lay myself bare for fear of him being turned off and then turning away, but above all this I had never known a male figure that loved me so unconditionally that he would allow me to make my own mistakes and still hold my hand throughout because He loved me that much. However this exact love which I so desired was there from My Father ready and waiting which had come through the sacrifice of Jesus Christ. To understand the height, width and depth of His love was to accept the unacceptable and I simply would not allow myself to receive and accept it because I did not deserve it. So I continued to punish myself by remaining alone. Despite the beautiful sounds of the worship music playing I was still in pain. Emotionally I was not free. I felt as if I was in a struggle that I could not share with anyone, not one single soul and certainly not God even though He was there waiting. I reflected on my day to day outward appearance to others where I would smile and say that I was fine, but in reality I felt lonelier than ever as I was left confined to the burden of my continuing pain. I could not even share with those closest to me how I was truly feeling for fear of judgement – something I was still having to endure from some of those closest to me; family members who could not deal with my difficulties and so would bury their heads in the sand seeking comfort in their own demons, and friends who had previously been a rock to me who without any explanation removed themselves from my life. It was hard to know who I was half the time or where I was so the battle I continued to fight was ongoing and filled with fear and confusion. I was in such conflict. I knew being a Christian, to claim or own any kind of fear and confusion was not that of God but that of the enemy. I also knew that one of the few responsibilities bestowed on me was not to worry about the actions or thoughts of others, but only that of My Father. I was not to worry about my life; what I would eat or drink, or where I was going because He was taking care of it. I was to focus on Jesus. I knew that my one and only fundamental responsibility was to place my life at the foot of the cross and to rest in Him and allow God to take control. I knew that my feelings in that moment were not relevant in the outcome of God's perfect plan for my life no matter how bad it looked because they were not the foundation for its success. I was to trust in the unseen...the not yet revealed perfect plan, so in knowing this I would have to stand firm in my faith and on God's absolute truth, waiting patiently for Him to work in my heart and mind so that I could be ready to accept His gifting in me. It was not for me to worry or work out the next step or the finer details to the script of my life, but to be the best I could be during my time of stretching and to wait on God's perfect timing. I was to face my fears by thinking the right thoughts, by doing the right thing and focusing on The Word of God and by not becoming distracted by the enemy's attempts to convince me that a life in Christ was a mistake. I knew that I was to rise up in my spirit even if the feeling had not yet followed by taking up that shield of faith because then, and only then, would I be fully equipped to deal with the ongoing and ever present battle between The Father and the enemy that plagued me with thoughts of self-doubt, fear, lack of confidence and insecurity. However, standing firm in fear was extremely hard for me, to the point of exhaustion as I did not have enough of the emotional resources needed to carry me, not even the smallest amount to allow me the breath needed to call out particular scriptures that would strengthen me in the battle. I was exhausted from what felt like a constant pressing down from my mind to my heart. I had spent many nights unable to sleep and many days energy deprived because of the ongoing battle in my mind and I was being stretched to my limit.

As a creature of habit and one who relied on the tangible, I had never been the best with patience and so I based every difficult episode, every decision and all understanding of any given situation simply on how I felt rather than taking it to God in prayer. I often sought out my own answers, looking in places I shouldn't rather than acting in obedience and waiting on God. Often I knew my disobedience would ultimately hurt me, but the continuous battle with my flesh meant that I ignored God's voice and did what I wanted in an attempt to get through the pain. There was often a feeling that I did not know any other way. I hated the discomfort and wanted to run away from it….after all that is what I had always done in the past. Whenever something felt difficult or I was being rejected or if something was taking too long, I made a decision to walk away. I would walk away rather than carrying my hardships to Jesus through prayer and by nailing it to the cross but despite not relinquishing control God had been speaking to me. In my very heart, He was still there. However, two weeks later

I still wasn't feeling any better. Nothing seemed to shift the feeling of rejection, sadness and disbelief over my continuing emotional burdens. I needed something different. I had become so fixated on 'Everything' that I could neither do anything nor see a way out. I was still not doing so well with my prayer life and seeking God. Yes I was praying, but the prayers were not as strong in their conviction as they had been before, because my prayers lacked sincerity. Something was missing and so I needed to get some tangible answers. There were times when I felt as if I were struggling to hear from God and so I felt as if I needed to seek those answers. It was time to move on and move forward even though I did not know how to. At this point I decided to meet with Pastor John to help me find what I was looking for. I was feeling apprehensive and unsure of what he might say, but as I waited for him to meet with me the feeling of apprehension began to lift and was replaced with an all too familiar feeling of peace. I sat by my window looking up to the sky as I often did. It was a clear sky; the sun shone brightly in the cloudless sky. I looked up and thought "Here I am Lord, what do you have to tell me? I'm waiting for you." I sat waiting in anticipation as my mind kept focusing on the words "Lord I am here, let me hear you" and in that continued moment of solitude, Pastor John arrived.

We sat and talked for about an hour where I explained to him how I was feeling, that I was struggling in thoughts of abandonment from God and that I felt as though He had forgotten about me and no longer wanted to answer my prayers. I explained that I remained in hope and prayer for the return of 'Everything' but I also questioned who God would answer if 'Everything' and my prayers were in direct conflict – him praying for someone else new and me praying for his return. I sat there unsure of my very own questions. As I babbled on clearly talking in a state of confusion, Pastor John did not interrupt me once. He simply sat there patiently as I desperately tried to get 'Everything' off my chest. He allowed me to talk things through, but as I looked at him I already knew the answers and the very truth he was about to speak from. He told me that as God's children we are free to and can make any choices we want. We can make a choice to love or not to love a person, put down past hurts and to let them go and that I myself needed to make a definitive choice to move forward. It was so tough to hear those words despite knowing he was right because I was so desperate to hear the answers I wanted, which was that God was going to bring my love back. It was an unrealistic expectation, but still the words came crashing down like a devastating blow. Whilst Pastor John spoke words of wisdom which I knew were led by the Holy Spirit, I couldn't take any courage from them. I felt defeated. He went on to say that there were things in life that should automatically bring joy, leaving behind nothing but peace and if not, those things needed to be let go of. He also spoke about God and His plans in the lives of His children, saying said that God always had a better plan. Pastor John went on to say that at times we may pray for things but if those prayers were not in alignment with what God had wanted for our lives He would not necessarily allow them. He then likened my situation to one of turning into a cul-de-sac and being stuck at a dead end. He said that the only way I could walk to freedom was by turning around and walking through my struggle and out into victory.

As I sat there with a greater amount of acceptance although still dejected, Pastor John went on to explain that whilst he understood my hurt and pain, God would give me the grace to get through it. He went on to say that God had seen my suffering and that I would not remain there forever. We also discussed the plans God had for my life, but with that Pastor John also went on to say that there was a very evident presence of the enemy trying to put a block on my blessings. He also said that when there is purpose in a life the enemy will try and stop it. Despite his encouragement, I still couldn't fully hear the message as I didn't want to accept that 'Everything' wasn't going to be given back to me. I couldn't drown out the disappointment which was building up in my heart, but then we began to pray. As he firmly held my hands to support me, we bowed our heads as I began listening to his leadership. I could feel a painful sensation in my throat as I tried to choke back the growing emotion and tears as Pastor John prayed for my release. My eyes were closed, but as I listened I heard prayers for my peace, grace and mercy and for God to help me to let go and as he used certain words in authority I could feel the ever growing presence of the Holy Spirit and a lessening of pressure. Following the prayer and after Pastor John had left, I realised the truth of the matter;

that God was not just steering me away from 'Everything' but to something better and that He had a wonderful plan for me which I could not yet see. My eyes were blurred to the vision. As much as I struggled with the idea, I understood that God never wanted me to suffer and that He wanted me out of the place of persecution and rejection that I had found myself in. The Father had wanted to see out the very best in my prayer life, spiritual life, in relationships with my family and friends, but mostly a deeper relationship with Him. I kept sensing the word 'surrender' and felt that my stumbling block was because I had still not fully entrusted my life to God. It was difficult for me because growing up I had learnt to do things my own way led by my feelings but now, as an adult Christian woman, I knew that I had to exercise another way that demonstrated growing closer to God and deepening my trust and faith in Him; as much as it had hurt going through my journey the reality of it all was that it was purely, truthfully and honestly God's will for me to have the very best because He loved me that much. I realised that if I wanted to have an earthly relationship filled with love and commitment meeting a certain criteria, there were things I would need to do and then God would grant it - that being fully accepting and letting 'Everything' go.

However it was still so difficult. Whilst I had continually prayed and spoken about God's place in my heart and placed Jesus at the centre of all things, my actions rarely showed that as truth. At times my faith was seemingly based on God proving Himself to me by giving me exactly what I wanted and when I wanted it – that being 'Everything'. However I didn't really understand that it was never about God having to prove anything to me and that yes, whilst he could work all miracles and do all things to turn something or someone completely around, my relationship with God should never have been based on Him doing exactly what I wanted on my timing. It was about having the courage to stand firm in fear by faith even when things did not feel as if they are working. Nonetheless, for so long 'Everything' had been my all and I had based my happiness on his part in my life. The truth was that whilst 'Everything' was a great love to me, I believed he could never be for me unless he accepted the truth of God's will. I felt that he too needed to surrender so 'we' could never be anything more than just another failed relationship statistic. I knew that it was a heart thing and both of our hearts were in different places which limited God's capability. I also realised that 'Everything' represented an important part of my life but his involvement could only be for a short period of time as God's rightful place was taken in my heart. Unfortunately, I had allowed myself to become stuck in a memory of a love that once was, rather than accept the love that was current. It was the essence of my fear in moving forward and the stumbling block for standing firm in the face of it. Nonetheless, moving on was about rising up and putting my best foot forward, standing firmly and only on my faith. I reminded myself of Hebrews 11:1 which said that faith is 'the assurance of things hoped for, the conviction of things not seen' (ESV) confirming for me what it meant to surrender to God and trusting Him in all things. It was this passage that reminded me of the truth that my faith could not be relied on by the visual, getting what I wanted and feeling as if my prayers were automatically being answered. It was not about that; it should always have been about having the courage to carry on even when things would feel so bleak.

More importantly for me was this; although I had been able to carry on in the past when things were seemingly beyond redemption to the point I could barely see far enough to plough through the pain, I still missed the mark. I had not yet firmly placed my spiritual feet on the ground, having the belief that God would do what He promised from the very beginning. I believed in God's power but because of a doubt within me and a deep rooted sense of being undeserving, I continued on in limitation. However my focus should never have been about what I thought of myself, but purely what God had always said about me and what I meant to Him. The Lord always knew that I had desires to be a good wife and mother and to have a kind, loving and successful relationship with a strong Christian man. However I also felt that He knew exactly what I could give at that time instead of propelling me forward prematurely. Also my source of encouragement had to come from the fact that I was to carry on despite seemingly not getting what I wanted. I knew I must remain true and strong even when it might have appeared that God was quiet. I was solely responsible for believing He would see His works in me through to completion but I realised during and after the accident I had never really done that and forgotten how The Father and I had come to the place we were in together. I had previously said I surrendered and believed, but I had not honestly done so because of my fears and so God was continuing on patiently waiting for me to realise the simplicity of what I had to do even though it felt so hard. The only way I could move forward and the only way that God could actually go to work in my life was when I fully released 'Everything' over to Him for good - released how much the pain had imprisoned me and released being stuck in a feeling of what was, because the past was behind me. It had gone by a long time ago. The enemy had tried so many times to break me down because unlike me, he could see God's vision for my future and wanted to stop it. I knew that he worked on my biggest fears and weaknesses, telling me the very thing I wanted I could never have because I was not good enough. I also knew that at times the enemy would send the greatest distraction centred on the things I struggled with which had been destroying my very life. He had tried to convince me of the worst and so I found myself faced with begging God to have mercy on my soul as I tried to fight against the enemy's schemes and in that moment I thought more about having the ability to stand firm in fear. My mind was then steered to some of the great men and women of The Bible (particularly of the Old Testament) who acted in total obedience to God's will because of their trust and unshakeable faith in Him; the likes of Abraham, Job, Moses, Isaiah, Daniel, Noah and the list goes on. Each of them took a stand on God's instruction and gave of themselves to The Lord despite not knowing the outcome of their lives. It was these very people whom I made reference to that made me sit up a bit taller and think about what I was doing. I took a further moment to pause in reflection, not relying on or worrying about anything. I looked out of my window and up to the sky and as I could feel the sun shining on my face, I could feel His warmth. Even though I had been in the same place before claiming an understanding, I could trust that little bit more. I still had no clue how I would get through any of it as my struggles still seemed to hold on but I knew that as I looked up to a powerful existence, I rose up in my spirit. I needed to complete my journey. With my feet firmly placed, shoulders back and head up I needed to be strong. I had always been a fighter and needed to fight back for myself through the help of the Holy Spirit. I no longer held the love from 'Everything' the man; I had love from God. It was a love that I needed, one that would make all my dreams come true but most importantly, it was a love that would set me free.

CHAPTER 16

I Rise

As I began physiotherapy and hydrotherapy along with all the
other regular trips to the hospital to start my rehabilitation, steadily
my foot started becoming stronger. I began noticing what felt like
miraculous healing as the swelling went down considerably within
the first week of treatment and I was able to do immeasurably
more in my mobility. It wasn't long before I was back to work and
teaching my fitness classes and although I was still in pain several
weeks after the accident, I was making progress. I began feeling
a sense of excitement and remained continuous in my thanks to
God that I was able to get back on my feet through His blessings. It
felt as if I were moving forward and that God was directing me to
a place of spiritual settlement as he demonstrated His faithfulness
through repairing me in the physical. I then thought about what
He might have been doing with me emotionally as I could feel a

difference in my way of thinking and how I was responding to thoughts or feelings connected with 'Everything'. For the first time in months I was able to not think about 'Everything' in a way that would allow him to overshadow my thoughts and I began to feel that God was directing me towards something else which took the focus away from myself and my own struggles. It was then that God placed a woman and friend in my life who through very evident similarities we shared a bond. My friend Amanda had gone through her own bereavements brought about by a difficult relationship and so we connected instantly. I could see in her a vulnerability which needed encouragement, but I could also see a definite strength and in that I wanted to help her. I didn't know what it was that I could do or what my actual purpose in her life was, but I felt drawn to her like a magnet.

I often spent lengthy time in prayer asking for God to reveal our purpose in each other's lives and for The Father to give me the tools to do His will. I began feeling led to remain in counsel with Amanda and so I began encouraging her to come to church. Within a short period of time she was making regular attendance and began to openly and confidently pray out aloud during worship. I began to witness her power as I listened to the congregation respond in agreement with her words, and although she confessed to difficulties in her confidence I saw her light begin to shine. It wasn't long before we became close, spending hours talking on the phone praying together and sharing our stories with each other. It was evident that we were both still carrying sadness connected with the loss of our relationships, but in our times of need we were able to encourage each other. It was then that I began to notice my own confidence grow spiritually as I was able to talk fluently about Christ, making reference to the many scriptures I had studied during my yearly devotional. I found myself surprised at the very things I was able to quote fluently when I had often thought my learning was limited. There were times when I had struggled to understand a passage of scripture or my mind wondered off to thinking about other things like what was happening through social media. There were even times when I would start devotional learning and become so distracted with a thought I didn't even recall the words I had just read – still God's words were within me, and not only was He in me but He was coming out of me in my sharing with others, especially sharing with Amanda. It was then that Pastor John began to encourage me to continue in support of Amanda by coming alongside her in discipleship. Nervous and somewhat apprehensive, I wasn't even sure that I was ready to take on such a responsibility, but I felt within my heart that God had spoken and I needed to listen in acknowledgment and trust His direction. It was then that I began leading Amanda through The Grace Course which I had attended the year before.

We would meet each Sunday after church where we would sit and go through the teachings, reading and learning together. It was then that she began to confide in me about other things

which she also struggled with in her confidence, which stopped
her wanting to read out aloud. I would look at her and feel such
an emotional pull to the things that she described to the point of
wanting to cry, but would not show on my face how I felt because I
wanted her to feel that she was in a safe place which was objective.
It was during that time of listening to her story in which I felt God
give me further instruction on how to lead and guide her. Instantly
I felt that The Father was not only helping Amanda through me,
but He was building me up for more responsibility. I began to feel
an even deeper passion ignite within me and it was then that I
began to pray in deeper counsel with God to reveal His plan for my
life in what I felt was directing me towards a path of some kind of
leadership. At first I felt stupid, convincing myself that I was foolish
to believe that The Father would not only use me but place me
firmly in a position as an encourager, propelling me to a place of
leadership over women. Nonetheless I kept hearing His voice in my
heart and feeling His presence through the Holy Spirit which often
was so powerful that when I felt deeply connected to it, the sheer
magnitude of it all would reduce me to my knees in thanksgiving
to The Almighty. I quickly learnt not to ignore His instruction and
as I became more sensitive to His will, I began noticing that I was
placed in a position to care for and pray over more women in need.
It wasn't long before I was completely distracted from any thoughts
of 'Everything' and I began to feel as if finally I was claiming
victory. He was no longer a point of reference or reflection and I no
longer desired him in the way which I had before. It felt as if he had

finally faded into the background and I was free to focus on myself and the work which God had given me to do.

The problem was that I had still forgotten something of great significance. Whilst I was moving comfortably towards a settled place of spiritual breakthrough, growth and development, the enemy was still lurking in the background ready to take an opportunity to attack. I had become desensitised to his very real presence and in my will to see God's work done, I dropped my guard. It was at that very point where the enemy struck again over my feelings towards 'Everything'. It was as if the enemy saw my breakthrough and progress, and in that moment put a stop to it with the very thing which was not only a weakness, but something which would destroy my very life. The enemy knew how to work on my fears and insecurities and despite moving on from 'Everything' he knew that to place any seed of doubt in my mind where 'Everything' was concerned would act as a catalyst for descending my thoughts back into chaos and sadness. I had greatly struggled with the idea of another woman having the heart and focus of 'Everything' because despite what may have been fact, a part of me still remained territorial over him. It made no sense as it had been well over a year since our separation and our life choices no longer concerned each other, but still I felt some kind of connection with him which made me want to protect him from harm.

I had no real concrete evidence of anything – just a real sense of someone else being in his life and I couldn't shift the thoughts from my mind. The feeling came almost out of nowhere as I kept sensing the presence of another woman. I began finding myself distracted with various ideas of what might have been happening with 'Everything' which continued to float around creating further distraction within me as I became less focused on my discipleship and the plans for my life which God had begun to reveal. I then found myself further tempted into thoughts that were not in alignment with God's word as I began to feel inferior to them. I tried to pray against the returned feeling of dread and anxiety, despite meeting with Pastor John to discuss various issues including how to establish and break down strongholds. I quickly identified the shift within me again as I became less positive about my own future, however I still remained in fellowship and discipleship with Amanda who was still going through her own struggles. There was a part of me that felt connected to my purpose, but another part of me felt as if I were lost in limbo. I couldn't talk to anyone to express how I was truly feeling for fear of being judged. Also I felt as though I was all out of resources because I felt that those closest to me who had been with me through my journey, would no longer have the patience to sit through another episode of my downward spiral where 'Everything' was concerned. So I felt I had no choice but to put on a brave face and go it alone. I continued to pray, but I could feel the attack on my mind growing. It made no logical sense other than a continuous looming presence and a reminder of an image in which I could see' Everything' with another woman. I tried all that I could to get him and the seemingly present "her" out of my mind, but I couldn't. In an effort to try and make some sort of sense out of my thought processes I tried to speak with my sister Faith but when I felt as if she did not understand my continuing struggles, I shut her out under the premise that I would work it out all by myself. However it was not possible and the reality was, at that point, I no longer had enough left in me to see through the hazy distraction of the enemy.

One evening I found myself driving home and my thoughts were consumed with 'Everything'. I felt confused and upset as without warning, there he was along with the memories of my love. I did not understand why or what had sparked off a sudden attack on my mind as it seemed unreasonable and certainly irrational to be overwhelmed, but I was. I began to cry and as the tears rolled down my face all I wanted to do was get home. In that moment I just wanted to get back to what had become a safe place and a sanctuary where I had begun to feel the presence of the Holy Spirit daily. I felt as if I was dying inside all over again and I was scared that I may not even have made it as I rushed back. The closer I got to home, the more desperate I felt as the feelings began to escalate. I began to question God over what was going on within me as I felt an all too familiar sense of having a panic attack loom. As I arrived home and closed the door behind me, I sat down on the sofa and cried out in anguish. I called out to God to explain to me what was happening within my heart and mind as I felt consumed with grief, but then the feelings turned into frustration and then anger towards myself for allowing a moment of weakness to consume me and so I continued to battle on in a state of despair and confusion as I tried to pray out my emotions. I cried out to God asking Him why He had allowed me to fall into the same trap and why He had not allowed me to finally be over 'Everything' and why He had continually allowed me to suffer the attacks of the enemy, but the biggest question was in my desire to know why The Father would not miraculously rescue me and wipe out any remaining love for 'Everything'. As I sat there my tears continued. I was exhausted, I was broken and I was tired of being tired. I cried out asking why over and over and the more I cried the worse I felt. I could feel nothing but hopelessness and in the deepening sense of suffering I begged The Father to just give me a break and that I truly could not stand another minute of the pain. As I continued to cry out, my voice getting louder, I continued to call out in prayer begging God to release me "Please Father God, please release me!" were my words as I rocked back and forth, head hung low as I tried to find some comfort. I couldn't breathe through a blocked and runny nose. I was a mess. I lifted my head and tilted it back in an attempt to retrieve some air and as I did so, I looked towards the cross above my door and an A4 piece of paper which I had stuck on the back of it. Some months earlier I had written a list of affirmations to help keep me focused at times when I felt less encouraged and as I looked at them suddenly I felt a calling.

I got up, still sobbing and barely able to breathe and I walked towards my door. I looked up to the cross and then back to the affirmations. I could barely make sense of the words and so I wiped away my tears in order to be able to see what was before me. I continued crying, but I managed to lift my voice and called out the name of Jesus. I begged Him to find and rescue me shouting out that I could no longer survive any more attacks and that once again I felt alone. In that moment I felt a sense of weariness and became light headed, but there was something that held me up and told me to read out the affirmations. I did not want to and I felt irritated by what I knew was yet another instruction from the Holy Spirit, but even though I did not feel like it I knew that I needed some help from somewhere and so I began reading each one out loudly:-

God loves me

God will answer my prayers

Jesus loves me

I will be happy

I will have peace

I will be free

I am beautiful

I will succeed

I will let go

God is working in my life

I will get through this

Pain is only temporary

My life will get better

I choose to believe God

Jesus will rescue me

As I read through the list of affirmations, barely able to speak out each sentence with any conviction, I felt a sense of the Holy Spirit tell me to just hold on. At that point I felt as if I could no longer remain standing as my strength felt as if it was leaving me, but I carried on. Blurting out each sentence through my tears, wet face and a running nose, I stumbled through to the very last one. As I read out the last few words Jesus will rescue me, I dropped to the floor face down and lay there with my arms covering my eyes. I continued to cry and call on Jesus asking for His mercy and rescue. I felt that I had nothing left to give, that all had been taken from me and I would never have the strength to carry out the works God had called me to do. I couldn't get up. I felt defeated and could do no more and so I lay there. I closed my eyes still sobbing, but suddenly I felt something. I wasn't sure what that something was and so as I remained with my eyes closed I continued to pray, and in that moment I saw a vision of myself lying at the cross of Calvary and suddenly all was quiet and peaceful. I continued lying on my floor, but by now my cries had lessened to the sounds similar of a whimpering baby as it self-soothed. I still felt a sense of sadness and so I continued to ask Jesus to comfort me and it was then that

I realised what I had been feeling. It was His presence in my very home, and there was no confusion that He had come to do as He promised and rescue me. I continued lying on the floor in what felt like a gentle conversation with my saviour. It felt as if I were laying at His feet and I felt humbled but mostly I felt a sense of love that instantly calmed me and as I continued to talk with Jesus I asked Him to strengthen me one last final time. I prayed for Him to lift me up from the very place in which I lay so that I would not only stand up, but rise up in my spirit. I prayed that He would give me such ambition, motivation and a focus that would see my testimony as inspirational to those who had suffered similarly as I had. I prayed that Jesus would take me to a new place; one where the place of the old had no hold over me and to a place where I would reign victorious over the very pain which had held onto my heart for so long. Not only that, but I would rise up in my belief that I was set free and, in that freedom, I would help to win souls for The Kingdom through my story. I continued lying there, telling Jesus that I would not get up from that place until He had strengthened every muscle fibre, every bone, every cell and blood vessel within my body....to the point of strengthening my very existence. Then, and only then, would I rise.

So I lay there, quietly being pacified by His presence. I wasn't ready to move as I felt peaceful and didn't want the feeling to end, but suddenly I felt His presence leave and then it was just me. I continued lying there thinking about growth and maturity and realised that I was more equipped to move forward than I had given myself credit for. Not only that, but I had the love of Christ which He freely gave to me when He went to the cross to save my very life. It was a life that I could no longer waste and had to seriously give thanks for. I had spent so long being pushed and pulled by the enemy's manipulation and it was time to stop and realise that I could and would do all things because I had an advocate in Christ to see me through to completion. I realised that, without a shadow of a doubt, all that I had been through was because I had great purpose; the enemy knew it, Christ died for it and God ordained it.

I thought about why my relationship with 'Everything' had truly not worked out. It was not because God had not meant for us to be in each other's lives, but as two people who were in Christ we had wanted our own way and were not fully motivated by the will of God because we were blinded by our emotions and feelings that were at times fuelled by the enemy. Along the journey I had begun in a place of not knowing and in not knowing I could be excused to a degree because I didn't know better, but once I had accepted Jesus Christ as my Lord and Saviour, it altered things. I could no longer say that I loved God and then place that love as secondary. I could no longer pray for blessings but compromise who I was by doing my own thing. I could no longer live a double life saying one thing but doing another because God, who was the author and finisher of my life, could see all things and knew the true intentions of my heart; and whilst it was because of a genuine love for the man who was 'Everything,' it was not because of a genuine love for

God, my Father, who was my true 'Everything'. I had remained in a relationship with a man where God had given me the freedom to exercise my own choices. I had been blessed with a light, but had forgotten how and why I had received that light. I had forgotten to be thankful, grateful and to act in a way that demonstrated a real understanding of what God had truly given me. I realised that God had always acted in a demonstration of love, and when He had asked for my cooperation in making the necessary changes to propel me forward for greater things, I ignored His leadership and guidance and it was for that reason that the very thing I loved the most had to be taken away. God had planned great works for me to do which involved a ministry in helping save the lives of many broken women, so in order for it to be realised there had to be radical changes. The truth was that if I had acted in obedience from the beginning, perhaps the journey would have been less painful but in the end, and despite the diversion, God was still leading me to the place He wanted me to be.

There was so much more to me than to remain as a broken woman, held back in mourning over the memories of a past love. Whilst my relationship with 'Everything' the man had been a significant part of my life, he was not how my story was to end. I was to go on and take the trials and tests which I faced during and after that relationship and turn it into an amazing testimony. My story of abandonment, lack of faith and fear of rejection is one that women and men suffer worldwide. My story represents and speaks to the women in need, women who are broken and women who are riddled with insecurity and blame, and with it cling to the hope of what was past, forgetting who they truly are; forgetting that they never walk alone. My story was not going to end there lying on the floor of my home; I was going to rise up and share it with those who may not have had the same strength to get through a painful loss. I was going to share my story with those who felt so beaten, that they believed there was no place to seek refuge. I was going to be that refuge. I was going to be the person who said that it was okay to make mistakes, because there was always an advocate standing in the gap for our freedom and that was Jesus Christ. I wanted to be the face of struggle and survival through to victory. I had never finished anything in my life but I wanted to see my epic journey in which had seen God bless me through to completion and whilst the journey had not turned out how I had originally planned, I knew it had reached its very best conclusion. I had been through an amazing transition. I had gone from not knowing Christ, to accepting Him, to turning away from Him, to being rescued by Him. There was no greater love and even though the road had been long and rocky in places, I had finally got to the cliff edge, taken a leap of faith and landed on the wings of eagles which were taking me home to the safety of the arms of My Father.

As I still lay there pondering the image of soaring high in the sky, I smiled. It was time to rise. I was ready and so I stood up from the floor. I didn't know how long I had been lying there but I knew that I was ready to get up. I felt calm and fearlessness took over my whole body. I wiped away the remainder of my tears, walked over to and sat down on the edge of my bed. I continued on in contemplation of what had just happened and as I bowed my head closing my eyes, suddenly I felt the presence of Jesus again. It felt as if He had returned to give me one final message and as I sat in anticipation of an instruction, suddenly I felt an awareness of His touch as He stroked my head and kissed me on the cheek. It truly was finished and I was set free. There was no questioning of it. I had finally surrendered because in that moment God had exercised His hand of grace, giving me the supernatural ability to walk away from my emotional imprisonment. He had removed my chains and unlocked the prison door and just at the point of what I believed was the impossible, He turned up just on time to show me how great was His faithfulness in His love for me. It was time to rightfully take His place in my heart as everything. There was no denying His timing. He had waited patiently for me to accept Him and for His love to be enough for me.

I was ready to allow God to be all that He needed to be and to readily demonstrate the depth of my thanksgiving to Him who had always been my best friend and the true champion of my heart.

CHAPTER 17

Everything

In the end there was Him, and He was my Father God who was everything. I loved Him and although I had not always known it or even accepted how important He was to me, it was The Father who had rescued me. Somewhere down the long and winding road of my emotions He had managed to repair my brokenness, bringing me to a place of spiritual excellence through His desires for my life. There was no longer a stop sign limiting my abilities through Him or His strength in me and I had finally reached a place where I was no longer afraid to go into the deep. In the past I had felt as if I were drowning in the sea of my emotions, but I came to be confident that God's love would always keep me afloat and that I was free to swim in the waves of the ocean despite any storm. He had captured each and every one of my tears and kept them safely in His care during my intense moments of trials so that at the appointed time He would reveal that He had always treasured them because I meant that much to Him. In truth it was through the many great trials in which my Father God had shaped and moulded me into the woman who came to a place of being able to remain standing and strong. It had not been an overnight transition but one which had taken place over a long period of time in which there was great sifting. Before I gave my life to Christ He was already there working, setting me up for the road ahead and although I did not know it at the time God had chosen me to do something of significance.

I first noticed God's hand of protection over my life when I was sixteen years old. I was walking home from college with my friends down a long and busy road which saw many cars and buses speed up and down it. I can remember the footpath on one side of the road being very narrow and just about wide enough for two people to walk side by side. If anyone walking along it needed to pass another person, it usually required stepping into the road in order to get ahead and back onto the pavement. I had always been alert whenever I needed to pass someone in this way, but on one particular day I became distracted in a conversation with friends as we walked along the busy stretch. I can only remember of the conversation that it was one centred around gossiping about a guy I liked and so my focus was totally on the subject matter. As I carried on babbling away, I stepped down off the pavement without looking back to see if any cars may have been coming and as I stepped into the road all I can remember hearing was my friends scream out my name. As I looked back over my shoulder, I felt the deafening beep of a double decker bus pierce right through my body. It had skimmed right past me, missing me by mere inches. I can remember feeling pulled by the vacuum of air that had been trapped between me and the bus as it sped past and carried on its journey. As my friends asked if I was okay I laughed off what had just happened, but I felt deeply embarrassed by my stupidity. I later realised on reflection that I had come dangerously close to have being hit by the bus and losing my life, but I recognised that I had not just been lucky – I had been divinely protected by God. It was again the same when I had my most recent accident; although I was hit by a car and injured, I knew that I had been protected from a far worse fate by an army of God's angels. I had been blessed by rescue not only once but twice, and so I knew that to be rescued in a situation which was potentially a matter of life or death meant that God had great plans for my future.

Although I did not recognise God's guiding hand over my life at the age of sixteen, He continued to lead me away from situations that were not for my greater good. I can remember another situation of great significance where God's discipline saved me from a life changing mistake. I had become romantically involved with a man by the name of David who, from the very beginning of our relationship, showed clear signs that he did not value me. I can remember believing that I had fallen deeply in love with him, so much so that I saw him as great potential for the future. I would often pray to God begging Him to change David and to make him love me, but God said no. At the time I felt frustrated and angry towards God believing that He never gave me what I wanted, but what I did not realise was that God knew exactly what I not only wanted but needed. He knew that David did not play a part in my future and not only that, but any part he did play would only steer me off the path God had intended for my life. I can remember at the time being inconsolable as I begged God through prayer to give me David's heart, but He did not move and eventually over time, I came to see exactly why. At the time it felt nothing short of punishment, but it was God's protection as he was guiding me towards His perfect plan.

Even though God had begun to reveal Himself, I continued on in my life making some very obvious mistakes. Although I often did not acknowledge The Father, refusing at times to have a relationship with Him, He was still there. He continued faithfully shaping and moulding me bit by bit, and when He knew it was time to move me forward He introduced a special man into my life who jumpstarted my road to freedom. It had always amazed me just how reliable God had been through His timing because He was truly never late. Not by a single second. Looking back over my life I can see very clearly the pinnacle moments in which God moved. On reflection of my relationship with God, through this story I came to know that His plan started to come together very carefully from the very beginning with each fine intricate detail mapped out. Each time I thought about the extent of His faithfulness and unconditional love, it took my breath away. When I reflected on my lack of faithfulness to Him and the fact that it never changed how He felt about me I felt overcome by his grace and mercy. God granted me a gift; a demonstration of His love through a beautiful relationship and that relationship saw God begin to move and change me for the better. Throughout the transition the progress was slow and although there was pain, it was through the pain that I saw and experienced God's greatest works take place. He took me - a woman who felt lost - and gave me a champion and through that relationship He began to teach me His ways. I struggled through as the lines became blurred between my love for God and that of a man, but still God showed me what it meant to love unconditionally. Despite God knowing that my love for Him was secondary to a man and despite Him knowing all of my faults and all my sins, He still continued to love and bless me regardless. Even through the rollercoaster of my emotions and actions which included blaming Him, still He remained close. God literally stood by me firmly despite my actions because of His divine promise to love His child. As the Father of Light He loved me perfectly, but He also disciplined me to my greater good as would any father who truly loves the seed he planted. There were times when God would not allow me to have what I wanted because I was not ready for it, and there were also times when He had to take things away because those things made me limit His capabilities and where He wanted me to be. There were times when God would allow me to fall in order that I would recognise He was the only one to get me back up, so that I would no longer lean on myself or anyone else but on Him completely.

In my growing relationship with God, I began to learn that He was continually speaking to me through various situations no matter how big or small and He reminded me that sometimes through suffering we discover the most valuable lessons. Over the years, but particularly the most recent, I found myself continually becoming ill with either constant colds or other ailments in my body. I couldn't understand why I was repeatedly coming down with different symptoms and whilst recognising my immunity was low, something else was happening within me. It reminded me that God was a part in all things leading and guiding me through. For every time I got a cold, couldn't breathe and felt weak God reminded me that He was the breath of life and that His strength was made perfect in my weakness and when I was hit by a car and physically broken; suffering intense pain and unable to walk, God lifted me up and healed me of a crushed spirit. He was very literally in all things a beacon of light and hope. He also taught me many things through my times of suffering. He taught me that I was still capable of loving, supporting, inspiring and encouraging others despite what I was going through myself. There were times during the early days of the breakup in which I struggled with wanting to face anyone, let alone teach any of my fitness classes. I would find myself in floods of tears not wanting to leave my home before psyching myself up just enough to get going. I would feel lethargic and emotional, but somehow God gave me enough strength to make my way. Once I got to work I would find myself feeling better and confident enough to stand in front of the class smiling and laughing. Somehow and quite literally out of nowhere my whole personality came to life as I looked out to the crowd of faces who in-turn looked to me for help through their fitness (or difficulties). In that moment I realised what God was doing; He was building back up my confidence by showing me that I was strong enough to lead His people despite my own difficulties. Not only that, but he was blessing me with a successful class as week by week the numbers of participants began to steadily grow. I also noticed a real sense of happiness and purpose whenever I would teach my classes despite how I was feeling in my own personal life and it was then that opportunities began to present themselves in the offer of teaching more classes. With each class in which I taught I began noticing that my ability to connect with the participants brought about greater success in my teaching ability which I knew was not by my own efforts because it felt so superior. God knew that I greatly enjoyed teaching and that I found much joy though it because I loved to encourage and engage people, and so He continued to bless me by developing my teaching ability to one of excellence.

In the growing recognition of God's intervention in my life, I felt a deepening desire to demonstrate my faithfulness to Him. I wasn't sure how I would do so in any great lengths, but I wanted to show Him that I was dedicated to His will. It was at this time that God lay something on my heart. One day whilst going into the women's toilet at work I felt disgusted by the amount of used paper towels which had been dropped and left on the floor. I felt annoyed by the many women who I felt had been somewhat disrespectful to the cleaners who would then have to pick up after them. It was then when I felt the presence of the Holy Spirit speak to me and say not to judge others, but to simply pick up the paper towels from the floor and place them in the bin myself. As I screwed up my face and pursed my lips in disgust, I felt the instruction grow stronger in my heart and so I picked up each used towel from the floor and placed them in the bin. After doing so, I left the toilet knowing that God had spoken but I thought that was it until He spoke again the next time I went to the toilet. Once again I felt Him lead me to pick up the paper towels and He continued to do so every single day for months. There was not a single time when I could go into that toilet without hearing God's instruction, and although there were days when I categorically did not want to pick up the rubbish I could hear the words "great is your faithfulness" and they would steer me on. I came to learn that again God was teaching me something about purpose and trust. He was teaching me that I needed to be committed to His leadership and He was also showing me that in order to be trusted with great things I would first have to demonstrate being faithful in the little things….so I continued on picking up those paper towels.

My closeness with God and desire for a deeper relationship continued to grow through prayer. I was already spending a considerable amount of time with Him each day and with it I began to notice that my desire for the Holy Spirit to grow within me began to build in intensity. As I asked for more of Jesus, calling on His name to reveal Himself in each and every part of my life, the more I noticed a shift in what took place during my prayers. Words would flow from me with an outpouring of abundance and I would see God place visions before me. As I prayed for deeper revelation and placed myself at His feet, I felt a connection to Him that was beyond explanation. In the past I had been in conversations with a friend who had asked me if I had encountered the Holy Spirit, but at the time I could never answer her with any form of certainty because I did not know if I had. The truth be told back then I had not because I was not open to it and it was only until I had did I realise its sheer power. When I first felt a direct encounter with the Holy Spirit through prayer, it moved me to tears. I felt such peace and a love which left me in no doubt of where it came from. It felt pure and like a powerful surge of energy had passed through me and made my whole body come alive. It gave me clarity, focus and a great deal of comfort, as well as a renewed sense of strength. Any time I felt God in this way I wanted to remain in that feeling for as long as I could but not only that, I wanted to share my experiences with those I loved and treasured who were closest to me. I wanted to try and be an example of God's love towards them because it was true that some had not yet experienced God in any real deep way and that some had struggled with their own battles. I wanted to show them that despite the struggles there was always love and a way to freedom and victory, and that bit by bit He could restore them just as He had begun restoring me by changing the way I walked and talked and how I viewed life as a whole. Many things I had previously placed a high value on became of no consequence as I focused just on God and where He was taking me. I felt fearless, courageous and sure of who I was shaping up to be by God's grace. No more did I whimper and cower away in the corner, thinking I was not strong enough to go forward into bigger and better things. I had begun to be bold and confident that God had moved away obstacles that were hindering me by replacing them with greater opportunities. I was also able to see the bigger picture, whereas in the past I only saw what appeared to be right in front of me. I became excited and filled with motivation to do God's work, and to receive more of Him day by day. I noticed that the more I sought after Him the more I desired Him, and soon enough it felt as if I could not survive a day without Him nor did I want to. God was the beginning and the end and became the lover of my heart and soul. It was Him that I wanted above it all because it was only God that had kept me alive and loved me through all the hurt and rejection of every failed relationship. It was quite literally God's constant love, which He lavished upon me, that saved my life. I had stood at the cliff edge on more than one occasion, but He was always standing right there with me. God had become the wind beneath my wings. He had not only encouraged me to take a step of faith, but He encouraged me to fly and with that He began taking me to places where I could soar.

One of biggest differences for me in my walk with Christ once I fully surrendered and let go, was that I no longer felt alone anymore. No longer did I fear the future because I knew that I could trust God to do the very things that He had promised. There had been many things which had caused me to feel hopeless in the past, and one of them was the outcome of my future once my relationship with 'Everything' the man ended. I had panicked because I felt that all hope of a future being a wife and a mother were forever dashed. I was a woman in her thirties, a Christian and carrying way too much baggage for there to be any chance of meeting anyone new. I would have to start again but not only that, I would have to start again with the odds greatly stacked up against me. I believed that it would be difficult and near to impossible for me to not only meet a good man, but a strong Christian one. I felt that any good man of a certain age and of substance would have already been taken and even if I did meet someone I liked, I had no guarantee that Mr Next would be Mr Right. I believed that to meet someone would have taken time….time that I no longer had on my side. As a woman of a certain age and having never been pregnant, I questioned the idea of my fertility being a factor as it was evident that any possibility of having children would become that much more difficult as I got older. However, during my time of questions and worry, God moved and again laid something else on my heart. He placed Sarah, the wife of Abraham from the bible before me. Sarah was an old woman and past the age of child bearing years but God used her to give birth to a nation and granted her and

Abraham a son, Isaac. At first Sarah had believed that it was not possible and had more or less given up hope, but God spoke and said "is anything too hard for The Lord?" The truth is that nothing had been too difficult for God from the very beginning - I just couldn't see it because I trusted my own understanding and not His promises, but it was those very words that kicked my mind and focus into gear and back onto Him. It had taken some time to see a change in me but God had been patient and through His patience and my willing I began to trust and lean on Him knowing that He would not leave me in the wilderness. It was through my growing faith that He was able to truly begin His great works in me which I knew was leading up to a spiritual breakthrough and a blessing which was beyond my wildest dreams. Each day I felt closer to Him and I could sense a growing maturity that saw me care less about matters that took my focus away from Him. I came to realise that as I released my faith more and more, God had begun to reveal exactly what He had been preparing me to receive through the great sifting of my life. It was then that I confidently and willingly surrendered my life along with the facet of my very being to His care, and began focusing on where He wanted me to be. There was nothing else I needed to do other than to continue in seeking His will for my life. I had been afraid to be alone in the past believing that any chance of finding love had been stolen from me, but that was not true. God knew who He had planned for me and so I was to trust that any good man who truly wanted my heart would go to God to get it, and that in due time the person would be revealed and there would be no doubt where He was sent from.

The freedom I felt when I finally let go of trying to control life by my own strength was revolutionary. It allowed for God to truly break down my emotional walls of feeling rejected, hurt, angry and depressed to a place of liberation. I realised something very important once I truly surrendered; I could never have given away something that I myself did not have and that was the ability to love the person God had created in me. How could I have ever truly loved without limit when in the past I had always looked at myself as limited? On reflection, it was only through God's grace and almighty strength that I began to change by taking the limits off and allowing Him to do in my life what needed to be done. There were things within me needing to be changed which would then unlock my capabilities and it began with changing my attitude towards God's place in my heart. I came to realise that He needed all of me and not a compromised version so that in all things I could truly be faithful in my dedication to others. In offering my life in service to God I felt the full magnitude of His calling. I began hearing from God and could recognise His guidance and divine protection as every step I took became stronger and landed in a placed of authority.

For the first time in my entire life, I felt awakened and as if I were seeing the true value of the life He had given me for the first time clearly with a fresh pair of eyes. There was a realisation which seemed to awaken my senses and I could hear God speaking into my heart which concluded everything:-

The Father had loved me from the very beginning and it was His love that determined the outcome of my testimony which sprung forth a tree of life. I had been planted at conception and with each year of my life I had been growing, sprouting branches and deepening roots with His guidance and love. Nonetheless there were changes along the way, which saw my evolution. There were seasons that saw me being stripped bare through trials and tests of faith, and there were seasons that saw me blossom through experiencing true love to seasons of shedding of the old where I had to give up and let go of the things that were no longer a part of me. It was a continuous cycle of change, but no matter what was on the surface, with the love of Christ and the very will of God saw my roots deepen. God nurtured those roots so that when the elements of everyday life came against me, I was able to stand firm. I saw God make me an unshakeable oak – one that also gave life to others. God had grown me up to be so strong that not only could I stand in a place of solidarity with The Father, but I was able to stand firm as an example of survival to others. Through my tree of life I was able to give people rest and support and for them to see beauty. God had made me so strong that I was no longer in a place where I could easily be cut down. I stood growing tall for all to see. I knew that I still might have shown scars where life experiences had been engraved on my heart, but it was through those scars I could be relatable to others. I knew that The Father had grown me to be a strong tree of life and it was through Him that I found my voice and was able to share my testimony through my story.

A wise man once told me that when I had allowed God to do what He needed to do in my life, I would undoubtedly have a powerful testimony. At the time I was broken and defeated and did not believe that God loved me enough to save my life from the suffering I felt, but He did. He more than rescued me – He completed me and made me whole. My life was fragile before God revived my heart, but not only did He revive my heart, He gave me the strength to get up and run my race to completion. I had not only run it, but I had won it and it was through blood, sweat and plenty of tears that I crossed the finish line. I won the race not because The Father had finished his work in me – His work had only just begun. Nevertheless I won the race because He continually loved me unlike any other. To find everything takes time and it's never without sacrifice but the reward is great. You have to close doors that you wish could remain open and you have to be willing to love enough to let go. You have to be willing to put your life on the line with no guarantee that when you jump someone will catch you and you have to trust that any end is just the start of a new and more amazing beginning. I am living proof of victory. I have been the lotus flower surviving in muddy waters remaining at ease and I have continued to be at peace because of God's rescue at Christ's expense and immeasurable favour. There had been times when

I would look at an image of the cross and could see the extent of Jesus' love for me. The cross symbolises the height, depth and width of His love which is sacrifice and I know that through it, there could be nothing for me to fear and no giant I could not conquer. There would never be a time where I would ever feel so low again, and I have spoken with great conviction knowing that I could never feel unloved because I have retained a love so superior it is beyond any comprehension. It is for that reason, I could never give up on God nor give up fighting for the very name that saved my life and that is Jesus Christ.

My heart remains forever open to receive and believe in God, and my faithfulness to Him will remain despite whatever may try to come against me. I have not only survived but I have been restored and I know that my strength to endure came only by the power of my Father God, who is everything. For every test there is a testimony and in life we do pick up scars, but it is God who heals the broken hearted and seals every wound. His timing in my life gave birth to revelation and a voice that will continue to be used to encourage those who have been hurt to a place of overcoming any obstacle and on to a place of victory. There has been no mistake that in the present moment God has moved in the hearts and lives of each individual who has read these words to completion and He will, as He has done with me, change the very existence of every man and woman who has read this story through to the very end.

Everything starts with you and will always end with God. He has called you by name because you are in Him and He remains in you. Listen and you will hear Him call out to you.

EPILOGUE

Letter to 'Everything' the man

Dear Everything,

God sent you. You entered my life and changed the very air that I breathed and gave me the most valuable gift I could ever have hoped for, and that was showing me the way to Jesus Christ. You never once forced me into anything as you understood that it was not about trying to convince me into a relationship with God. You always supported and encouraged me and allowed me to see God's work through you by always acting in kindness and love. I thank God for your life because despite it all, I know of its truest value. I know you have been ordained for greatness and even though you have walked through some dark valleys, your light will ultimately shine for the greater glory of Our Father and I will celebrate in your victory for that day will surely come. I know that our relationship did not survive for a number of reasons but despite struggling at times through many difficult thoughts as to why we failed, I know that there was a time when you truly did love me. At times it had been difficult to hold on to that fact, especially as I felt you had walked away so easily. There were times when I had felt you had lied to me and I resented you for that. I never hated you, but I found it difficult to see you as God had always seen you and I struggled to truly forgive you for the pain I felt you had caused. I know it was never your intention to hurt me; nevertheless I did experience a great amount of pain but only because I loved you that much. What I am saying is not to blame you, place you in a position of shame and regret, or to make you feel bad, but a part of my emotional healing has come from being able to tell you honestly how I felt the day you left me. At first I was angry because I felt that all you had promised you took away without giving me a choice or an opportunity to try and put my mistakes right with you. I remembered a time when we sat in my car when a situation forced us into a make or break situation and you promised to stick by me and love me no matter what....do you remember? It was for this reason why I remained in our relationship even when there were times I thought I wanted to leave you. I stayed because I held on to a promise, but also because I truly believed that God had brought us together for a purpose and so I was going to make a choice to stick by you no matter what. However, I realised that I had carried around the baggage of a broken promise for far too long and that releasing it and moving on had been far overdue. I want you to understand something; I forgive you and I thank you for providing the very tools for my salvation. You had always said that you wanted to see my relationship with Christ grow on its own merit and despite the way it happened, you were the reason and the season that ignited a gift that started everything. I can never thank you enough for being that man in my life because the man I met and came to know was a true gentleman, my hero and a person with great integrity. We have all had a past which sometimes can affect our actions in the present during moments of weakness, but I had known you….truly known who you had been in Christ and that the calling on your life could never be erased. God is and will always be absolute truth and you were his demonstration to me of that. There were indeed times during our breakup where I felt as if you had always been a stranger and that I had never truly known the real you, but then I would be reminded of who God had always revealed you to be –a man with an ability to move mountains. I had seen it with my very own eyes and so that could never be a lie. Some people might say that I was blinded by love or under an illusion but it was not that and I could never have come to the place of where I am had I not met you. We met purely because God had intended for us to be in each other's lives with purpose, but for what, I am not sure of or even if it was ever fully realised. However, I know that the true man in you who may struggle at times (as we all do) is the man who God has His finger firmly planted on and He has called you by name and your time is coming. You have also been blessed with great strength, but your physical strength is only a reflection of your spiritual strength if you will only truly let God into your heart and allow Him to transcend your very being and not simply fade into the meaningless. You have the ultimate advocate who stands firm for you and that is our Lord and Saviour Jesus Christ. He is the only love that you will ever need and His love will set you free. I have learned of this and the power it gives me to have not only survived, but to have gone on to soar to excellence through a great and endless love. I want you to know that all is well in me. I have finally been set free by God's love and I am happy and so I am sharing this with you as I know you would want to know of my victory through Jesus' great and sacrificial love. I am no longer in a place of sadness over losing you because in losing you I found my way into the arms of Our Father where He has protected and guided me to a love that has at last completed me. He has satisfied my soul and for me there is no longer a fear over what was and what is to come. Our Father God has sharpened my faith and assured me that He will do in my life what He had promised from the very beginning. His arms have always been wide open and so now there is no place I would rather be….at last. I pray that God will mark your heart in the very deepest of places so that you too will fully rest in Him. We both have our own journey in which God has firmly placed us towards with His righteousness and we know instinctively but mostly through acceptance that His work will be seen through to completion. I am just so grateful that He has never let either one of us go no matter what we have faced or how bad things have been in the past. We know that at times there may be pain in the night but joy always comes in the morning; so my prayers for you are to see the branches of your tree flourish and that any place you decide to put your feet will be on solid ground and not in a place which might take your focus away from God. I never understood the calling upon your life and I certainly did not believe in the calling on mine, but we have both been called to be free and to be world changers. It is for this reason why we celebrate and acknowledge that Our Father, and Our Father alone, will always and forever be all that we ever need and our one true everything.

From your Sister in Christ,

Janine

Lightning Source UK Ltd.
Milton Keynes UK
UKOW06f1012250615

254049UK00001B/100/P

9 780993 299605